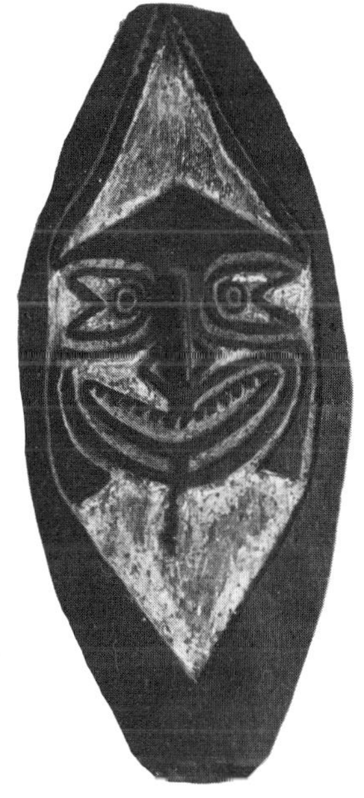

Aboriginal and Oceanic Decorative Art

The Travelling Art Exhibition is an extension service of the National Gallery of Victoria which aims to make the Gallery's collection known to a wider public and stimulate an awareness of many forms of art in country areas. As evidence of this variety, the four previous Gallery travelling exhibitions have focused on abstract elements in Australian painting, Melbourne figurative painters of the 1950s, and Asian Art and Textiles.

The travelling exhibition is designed for extreme flexibility and mobility. The complete exhibition, with its own lighting fixtures, is transported from town to town in a specially designed Bedford van. The paintings and artefacts are already fixed to hessian screens providing the advantages of protection of the art works and ease of erection, the screens with their tubular supports being capable of transforming a church hall into an attractive exhibition room.

Foreword

The decorative impulse is an important element in both Oceanic and Aboriginal art, which, like a hydra headed organism, can take many forms. The artist's decorative motifs, like his materials, pigments and tools, are drawn from his environment and art is born of this natural harmony which also embraces religious beliefs and rituals.

Sepik art is restless in its vigorous transformation of human and animal forms into sculptural images often fraught with uneasy distortions. Seething shapes, angular projections and convulsive curves are thrust from a blackened chasm of fears, threats and desires expressive of the human condition. So a shrunken human body is overpowered by a great slanting proboscis, suggestive of sexual aggression. Even utilitarian objects, like sago pounders, become vehicles for dynamic figurative carving rather than grimly functional implements; and the villager's daily existence is enriched as a result.

Massim carving, by contrast, operates on a two dimensional plane exhibiting a delicate balance between line and mass. A lime spatula is a graceful symbol of masculinity; its shiny black surface etched with flowing white wires of curves.

Similarly, the art of the Solomons is often a rarefied monochrome dance of spidery linear elements; the ornament being carefully orchestrated to complement structure, like ivy growing on an oak. So, deep black food bowls in bird or animal shapes are speckled with discreetly arranged pearl clusters or silent, circular giant clam shells are overlaid with spiky skeletal turtle-shell motifs. Even the humble fish hook is a glistening pearl surface decorated with tiny bobbles of beads.

If Solomons art is a series of elegant black and white duets, Aboriginal bark narratives resemble quartets composed of the natural earth pigments of black, white, red and yellow ochre. Nature is freed in a geometric mosaic of earth coloured shapes echoing tribal myths rooted in the land. Cross hatched patterns chase across the strips of dried stringy bark, or enliven the surfaces of bodies and rocks with sacred symbols. Outline, image and colour are bold and raw in this literature of simple visual images, reverberating through a rainbow of brown nuances the story of a people.

Judith Ryan
Circulations Officer
National Gallery of Victoria.

Introduction

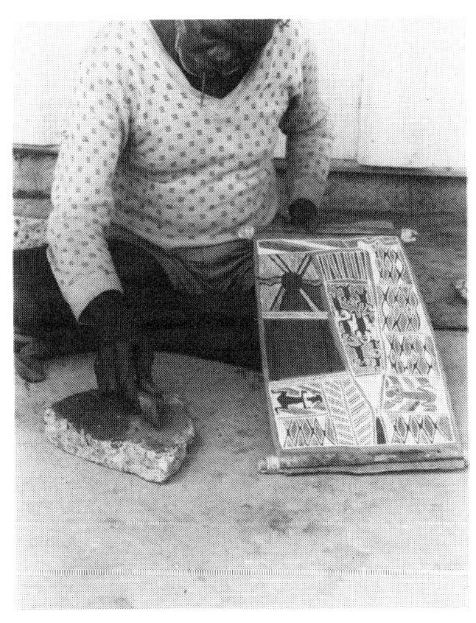

Mungurrawuy leader of the *Yirritja* Moiety painting a picture of a tragic circumcision ceremony.

Several years ago, in North East Arnhem Land, I stood with my old friend Mungurrawuy of the Gomaidj on the summit of the sacred Wyal rock (Mungurrawuy's 'Dreaming') on Mount Saunders and looked to the west across Melville Bay, where Captain Matthew Flinders had encountered the Macassan trepangers under the command of the serang Pobassoo, on February 17, 1803.

Mungurrawuy's ancestors have lived in this pleasant locality for thousands of years, performing their great ceremonies, hunting and fighting, and living in perfect harmony with the land. The *Yulngor* were there centuries before the pyramids were built, and centuries before man penetrated the Americas. After all these years of *Yulngor* occupation, between the rock on which we stood and where Flinder's ship rode at anchor 176 years ago stands the new *Balanda* (whiteman) town of Nhulanbuy, the fourth biggest town in the Northern Territory, set in the heart of an Aboriginal Reserve declared 'inviolate' in 1931.

Mungurrawuy said 'This mining company he is going to push im up all that fella tree. No possum, no goanna, no kangaroo, no tucker for me. If this had happened before the missions we would have killed that fella *Balanda*'. I turned and looked at my old friend, saw the distress in his face and realized I was witnessing the final destruction of an ancient, mystical, non-materialistic culture that was probably the oldest in the world; having taken 40,000 years to develop and less than fifty years to destroy.

The 'homelands' movement, funded by the Government, has resulted in approximately sixty per cent of the *Yulngor* moving away from missions and settlements to their tribal lands, which has led to a limited revival of the ancient culture. A crisis will be reached when men like Narritjin, Mungurrawuy, Yangarrin and a few others 'finish', if their sons are unable to live according to their choice by the 'old law', on their tribal lands.

Few Australians have really experienced the North in a meaningful way. It entails living off the land with its abundant supply of geese, duck, fish and vegetable foods known as 'bush tucker', cooked in the ashes; and hearing, on the flood plains, the beat of a thousand buffalo hooves, or the roar of the North West Monsoon with its lightning and thunder and torrential rain together with cyclones and water spouts. This is a terrifying time as the storm 'boss' *Djambawul* hurls his *larrpun* (spear) to form flashes of lightning and bangs his thunder clubs together. On a still night, the drone of the didgeridu beats out the rhythms of the *Walika* and the *Leera,* the most ancient rhythms in the world, and old song cycles are performed whose origin goes 'back and back into the 'Dreaming''. Imagine witnessing a turtle increase ceremony and hearing the chanting performed to liberate the life essence to enable the turtles to breed, as in the Turtle Increase Ceremony Chant:

> The long necked turtle floats
> In the blood red sea of the 'Dreaming'
> Casting the age old brown shadow
> On the sand below.
> We have seen him like a green shadow
> In the great depths
> We have seen him moving in his shell
> Through the mangroves like an old man.
> We have seen him resting and feeding
> Under the water on the weeds
> That grow on the great sandbars
> We dance the hunting of the turtle
> We dance the paddling
> The foam and the waves.

The chanting of Aboriginal poetry resembles the singing of Gregorian chants and, like the dances and the art, is intimately linked with their religious beliefs. Certain chants telling a story consist of couplets composed in a very sophisticated manner which enable each separate couplet to make a complete statement in itself.

Eagles Soaring (Translation by
permission of the Strehlow Foundation).

Near the sky's soft flesh
In the air they float;
Splinters of the sky
In the air they float.

Breast plumes gleaming black
In the air they float;
Near the sky's soft flesh
In the air they float.

The Yulngor World Before White Contact

When the *Yulngor* Clans arrived in this area so long ago they settled around the source of life — the water holes. For in and around the water holes they found all manner of food and materials that supplied fuel and fibre. In the course of time the food plants around the water holes and the animals and fish in the area became totems of great spiritual significance.

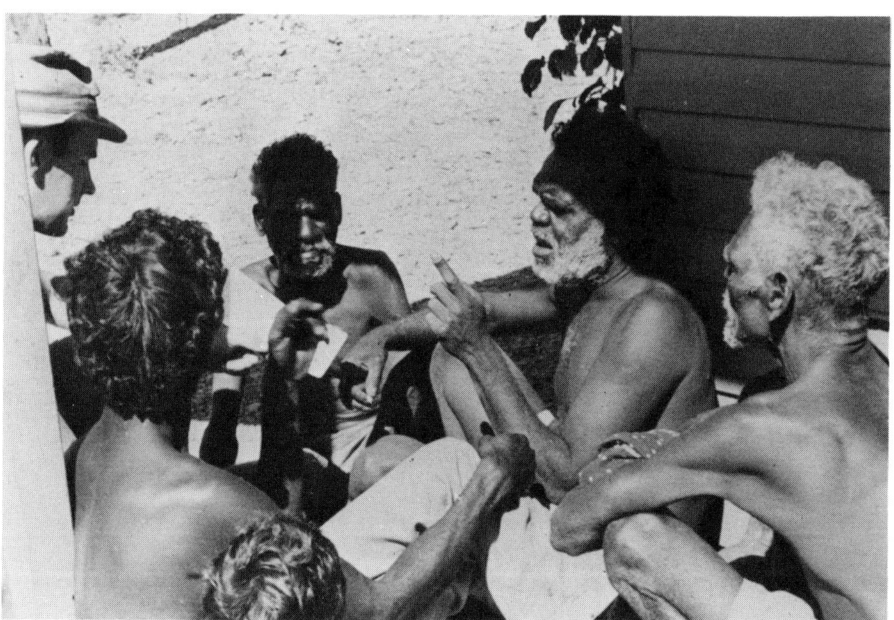

And 'in the Time before Morning'.

Totemic symbols were carved in wood, made of paper bark, painted and decorated with Banyan bark, string, feathers and bees wax, and were known as *rangga*. These symbols were used in increase or fertility ceremonies and some totems were circulated among the clans as an invitation to take part in an important ceremony. Totems played a most important part in the initiation of young men when the branches covering the *rangga* were removed one by one, accompanied by the sacred chants, and finally the youths were told to open their eyes. As they stood looking at the *rangga* their significance was explained, and on completion of this ceremony the initiates had advanced one step along the path to being a *Ngarra* man. Totems are classified into two groups — *'garma'*, or low totems, which may be seen by all and *'mariian'* which may only be seen by fully initiated, old men, known as *Ngarra* men. An individual was referred to as a goanna man or a shark woman, ad infinitum. If an emu man ate a portion of emu he would commit a serious breach of totemic law for which harsh penalities were imposed.

Tribal Aboriginals lived in a spirit world and the spirit ancestors were everywhere. In the water holes was the wind and when the leaves of a tree rustled it was *Mangelcaw*, the Tree Spirit, speaking. They believed they lived in their own special world which had been made for them by their spirit ancestors 'in the Time before Morning' when they awoke from their great sleep and called upon the sun to rise. They believed they were of the land and that the land owned them and not they the land. In their eyes the whole country was a spiritual landscape and its important features were 'Dreamings' preserved by myth and chants. Apart from the totemic ancestors there were numerous lesser ones such as *Kandarik*, the Kangaroo Man and *Minyaba*, the Turtle Man. These supernatural beings could assume the form of the totem they represented, at will. Sometimes *Minyaba* would appear as a turtle, sometimes as a man. These totemic beings also made the law dictating how the turtle would be hunted and, when caught, how it would be cooked.

The *Yulngor* were very secure in their beliefs because for thousands of years they had lived in harmony with nature and, in the same manner as the Red Indian of North America, believed that the mountains and the rivers never die; for as long as the rocks and water holes were there, life would go on. The intrusion of the white man into the scheme of things was devastating. The young men admired the material possessions of the white man and came to reject the rigid discipline of tribal life, causing much friction between the old men and their sons.

The Arrival of The Balanda (White Man) and the Japanese

In Arnhem Land, the white contact occurred much later than in other parts of Australia owing to the remoteness of the area and the lack of roads. In 1907 the Macassans from the Celebes, who had visited these shores for several centuries gathering trepang, were prohibited from visiting Arnhem Land and the Japanese pearling luggers began to arrive on the coast. They treated the *Yulngor* badly and on a number of occasions Japanese were fatally speared. In 1932 a number of Japanese were killed at Caledon Bay. So remote was this spot, that the news did not reach the rest of Australia until the following year; and, until it did, few Australians had any interest in, or knew anything about, North East Arnhem Land.

Mission stations had already been established at Goulburn Island and at Milingimbi in the Crocodile Islands, but these were 200 miles away and off-shore. At this time, white contact was minimal. The coast was visited by a few white trepangers and pearlers in small luggers. Fred Gray, Bill Harney and Horace Forster were among the first comers. For a while, the killing of isolated white men increased and in 1933 five white men, including the policeman McColl, were killed. There was continuing trouble between the *Yulngor* and the Japanese, and Government concern at the situation was only relieved when the Methodist Society offered to send a missionary into the area.

In 1935 Rev. Wilbur Chaseling (twenty-four years of age) and his young wife were establishing the mission at Yirrkala. With mail and supplies arriving at three monthly intervals, a language to learn, a home to build, a hostile people to pacify, gardens to establish and buildings to erect, he set about the herculean task with gusto and found time to make the first collection of bark paintings from this area, some of which are housed in the National Museum of Victoria.

James Davidson
Collector of Aboriginal
and Oceanic Art.

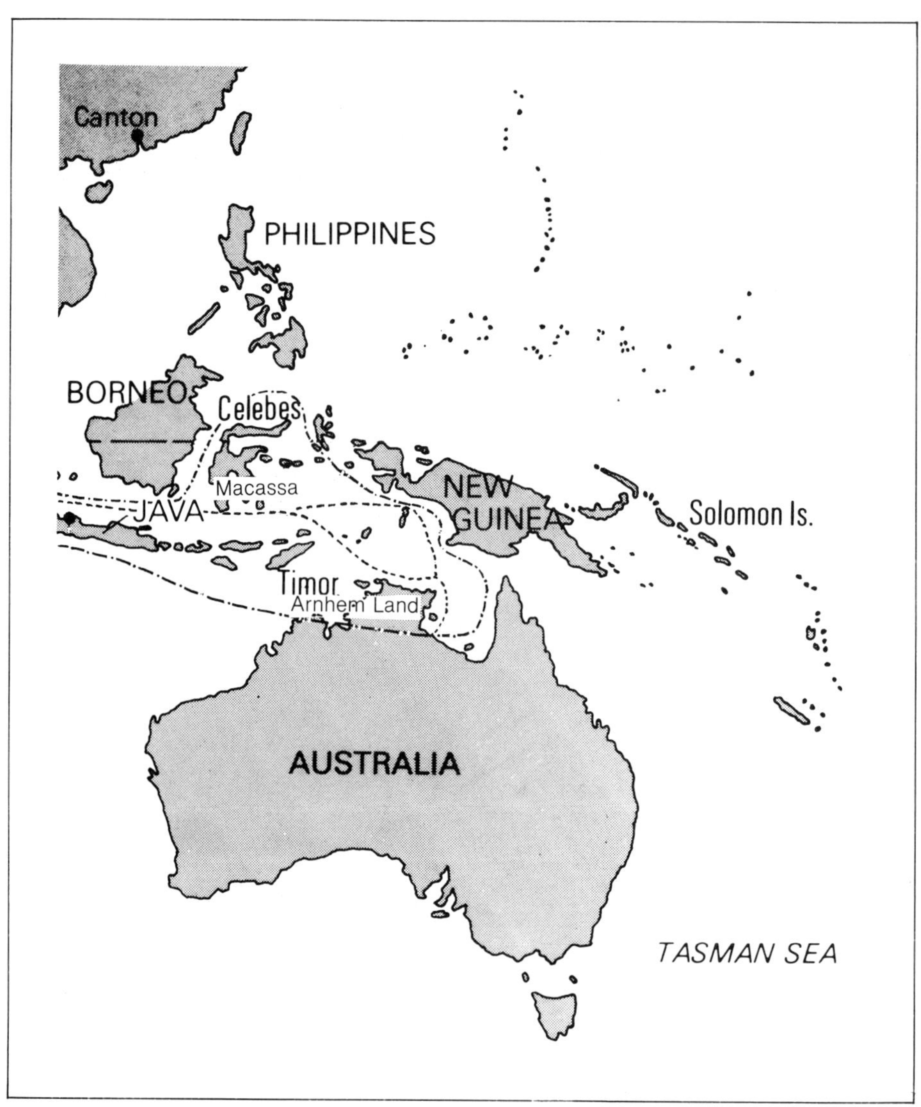

Outline of the world known to the *Yulngor* of Arnhem Land at the end of the Macassan contact.

Trade Routes to the North Coast of Australia.

Aboriginal Bark Paintings of Arnhem Land

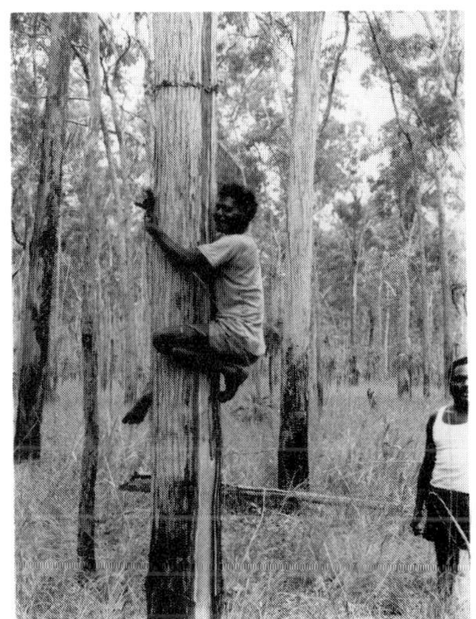

Butjiya making the top cut for stripping bark.

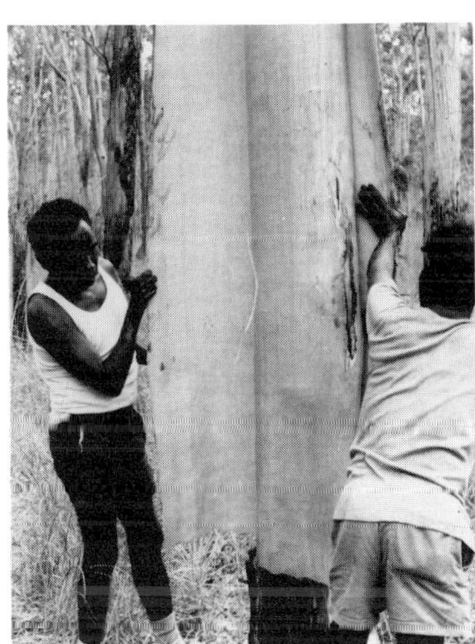

Gawarrin and Dutjiya — stripping bark.

About twenty years ago there came to Yirrkala, in remote Arnhem Land, a letter addressed to the Aboriginal artists living there, written by Picasso. It said: 'I admire and envy you your art'. Since then the work of Mawalan, Madaman, Birrigidji, Djawa, Dawdi, Malangi, Yirrwalla and many other *Yulngor* artists has captured the attention of the international art world. For this is the art of a people whose occupation of this area has been established at 40,000 years or more. The art is unique, in as much as it is one of the oldest primitive arts surviving in the world today. In addition, anthropologists have long considered the *Yulngor* to possess the most complex social structure amongst all native peoples. This is reflected in the complexity of their art. The bark paintings, as well as being the art of the *Yulngor,* are also their theology, history, and literature.

These paintings are executed on a sheet of bark, stripped from only one type of tree; the Tropical Stringy Bark (*Eucalyptus Tetrodontus*). Immediately after the monsoonal rains, when the sap rises freely, bark is stripped from carefully selected trees. As much as a whole day can be spent in looking for a tree with the right stripping qualities. Trees are tested by stripping a narrow piece of bark about five centimetres wide up the side of the tree. When a suitable tree is found, a top cut is made on the circumference of the tree, about six to nine metres high to wherever the first branch is encountered. A vertical cut is then made and the edges of the bark lifted, and pressure applied until it just 'pops' off the trunk, without any splitting, or fracturing. The bark is passed through a fire for about twenty minutes to steam it; at this stage it is very flexible and can be easily cut to size with sharp knives. It is dried in the hot sun with sand and weights on it for three weeks, and then the burnt areas are cleaned off the back with a large knife. The smooth side of the bark is rubbed with the juice of a crushed orchid bulb, a second coat of orchid juice is mixed with ochre and applied to the whole surface. When this is dry, the surface is ready for the artist. Brushes are merely a few strands of human hair, or a chewed twig, while the palettes are a slab of stone.

The pigments are ground from manganese and charcoal (black) limonite (yellow) hematite or ironstone (red) and kaolin or clay (white). The ochres are held under strict order of tribal ownership, the *Dhuwa* Moiety owning white and black and the *Yirritja* Moiety owning yellow and red. These laws are not taken lightly. Narritjin shares with Mungurrawuy complete ownership of the yellow ochre deposits near Yirrkala, which were discovered in the 'Dreaming' by the *Yirritja* Goanna Man, *Bitji*. Ochres are traded between artists who must qualify ceremonially for the privilege of using colours belonging to the opposite moiety. Rarely are more than four colours used in a painting (sometimes only two). The aesthetics of the work depend entirely on form and design.

The works of these artists are closely linked with ceremonial song cycles and dances miming the deeds of the great spirit ancestors of the 'Dreaming'. These spirit ancestors brought the laws to the *Yulngor,* and in North East Arnhem Land they brought the mala designs, gave them to the clans and told them their meanings.

Classification of Styles

As recently as fifteen years ago there were five utterly different styles, closely related to the areas in which they were produced.

1. **Groote Eylandt**
   The first barks were collected on Groote by Fred Grey, in the 1920s. With Bill Harney, he was one of the first white men to trade along the Arnhem Land coast.

The paintings were never very big, being approximately fifty to seventy centimetres long by thirty to forty centimetres wide; occasionally one would turn up about one hundred and thirty centimetres long by sixty centimetres wide. Nearly always the background was black, as manganese was easily obtainable; in fact in many places manganese pebbles covered the ground. The designs were built up with a series of short parallel dashes and represented a variety of themes. Being an animistic society, a large variety of totemic flora and fauna was depicted. Ancestral beings, sacred sites and hunting scenes were common. Very interesting abstract symbolism represented the North West Monsoon, and the South East Trade Winds.

This form of art disappeared almost overnight when mining for manganese began on a large scale about 1966. The art produced from then on suffered a great transformation and was influenced by Aboriginal visitors from North East Arnhem Land. Until 1965, Groote Eylandt Aboriginals had lived in isolation with minimal contact with Europeans. The fortnightly DC-3 and the odd supply ship for the Mission Station were the only contact with the outside world. However, like other parts of Arnhem Land, there was evidence of Macassan contact and Japanese pearling luggers visited before World War II.

2. **Bathurst and Melville Islands**

The tribes of Aboriginals living on Bathurst and Melville Islands regarded themselves as superior to the mainland people and called themselves the *'Tiwi',* meaning 'the people', as a mark of superiority.

The *Tiwi* have lived in complete isolation from the mainland Aboriginals for an unknown period of time. This very considerable time span of thousands of years is expressed by the art forms unique to the *Tiwi,* by their social mores, which by comparison with the mainland Aboriginals include the higher status of women, radically different burial customs and differences in their mythology. The time span is almost beyond comprehension. It is very evident that alien contact was practically non existent. Even mainland Aboriginals were reported to be killed if they visited these shores. Hart (1930 p. 170) states 'until the advent of white man, the Bathurst and Melville Islanders were not aware that any other people existed but themselves.' However it seems reasonable, in view of the contact in North East Arnhem Land, that now and again some Malay praus from Macassar in the Celebes, during the North East Monsoon, would have been blown off course and made landfall on these shores. It is certain that these visitors would have been killed or driven away. This hostility is probably the reason the Malays were unable to establish themselves on these Islands, as they had done in North East Arnhem Land, with a resultant cultural impact on the *Yulngor* of that region. The old men of the *Tiwi* do not remember the Malay fishermen visiting their country, and Campbell (1834 p. 143) said 'the Malays were never seen near Melville Island' and later (p. 155) 'Malay fishermen were forbidden by their *serangs* to go near Melville Island alleging it was infested with pirates'. In the early part of this century the *Tiwi* were still very warlike, and hostile to strangers.

As a result of this long period of isolation, *Tiwi* art forms differ completely from the art forms found on the mainland. Although some designs on the bark paintings bear a certain resemblance to rock carvings found in central Australia, the all important sacred symbol of the concentric circle does not occur. This style of bark painting is completely abstract in form, and unlike other forms of bark paintings, it is impossible to decipher the meaning of the symbols without the artist's assistance. For instance (Mountford plate 48 c. 1958) the Rainbow Spirit, *Maratji* at *Kulimbini,* is depicted as a large black circle in the centre of the bark, with bars radiating from it, and many smaller circles in red, yellow, and white displayed seemingly at random, on a carefully cross hatched background. Although in 1954 Mountford was able to make an extensive collection of bark paintings from this area, traditional bark paintings are now only occasionally painted by a couple of old men, and are therefore very scarce.

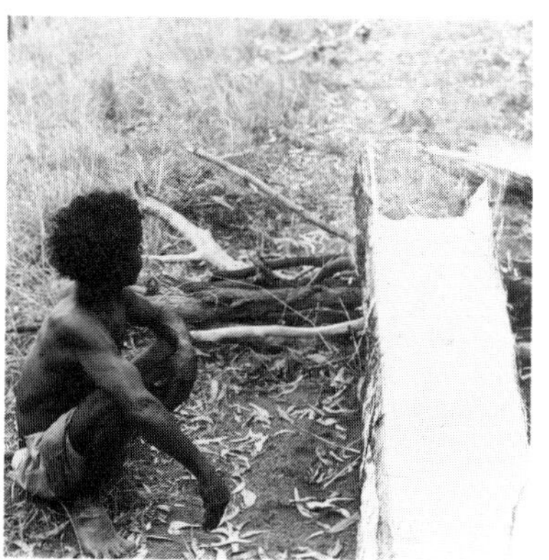

Mithili — steaming bark in fire to flatten it.

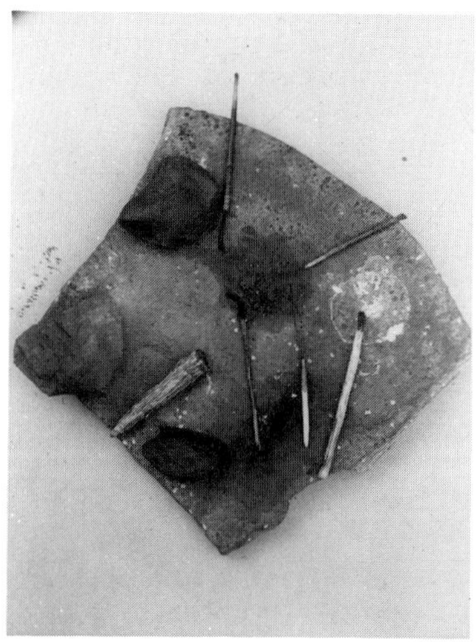

The bark painter's palette.

3. **West Arnhem Land**

Bark paintings in this area are closely related to the ancient cave paintings, and although the so called X-ray art has been reported among other races in the world, it is in West Arnhem Land that it has reached its highest state of development. Considerable anatomical knowledge is shown by the older artists like Yirrwalla, Gabagu and Nguli Nguli. The traditional artists even showed the crossed optic nerve in their X-ray paintings. Many of the cave paintings were produced on bark at certain times for the instruction of initiates, and for the guidance of body painters. The ownership and usage of designs and symbols are controlled by strict laws, and death by spear would result if the unthinkable arose where an artist made unlawful use of a theme, or symbol. Totemic subjects are often depicted — in both flora and fauna. Some paintings relate to the activities of cultural heroes — for example the Kangaroo Man, *Kandarik,* who in the 'Dreaming' originated bark paintings in this area. He decreed that when preparing for the *Ubar* Ceremony, kangaroos should be painted on rocks adjacent to the ceremonial dancing ground, and if rocks were not available that the kangaroos should be painted on sheets of bark. Often depicted are *Wintjili,* the woman who hated men but loved dancing, and would dance with men until they were exhausted and then killed and ate them, and *Mamaragan,* the Lightning Man, and countless others. The *Gunwinggu, Barada,* and *Gunavidji,* of West Arnhem Land had more good and evil spirit people in their mythology than any other clans, and the artists entitled to do so used these subjects in their paintings.

In a separate class were the paintings made by the 'clever-men', or sorcerers showing anthropomorphic beings. These paintings were used by the men who produced them, in the practice of black magic. The painting of a 'debbil-debbil' (evil spirit) and the singing of associated chants, would ensure that the evil spirit would harm a certain individual. 'Clever-men' were commissioned to act on behalf of aggrieved individuals.

Astronomical bark paintings were made throughout Arnhem Land, and Aboriginals all over Australia had a far greater knowledge of the night sky than most white men. This is an indication perhaps, of their deeply meditative and spiritualistic philosophy, of which ample evidence is observed when in close contact with tribal Aboriginal friends of long standing. 'Man is more than his tools, and what he eats, and the depth of 'savage' spiritual life provides challenging food for thought'. (Mulvaney, 1971, p. 12).

Although now painted on bark, the *Mimi* figures originated from the so called *Mimi* cave paintings consisting of artistically drawn single line figures. They were depicted hunting and fighting amidst showers of spears. Some had elaborate head-dresses and carried goose wing fans, spears, woomeras and dilly bags. Their main theme was man in action. When the white men asked the Aboriginals who had painted them, they replied 'the *Mimi* painted them'. Although Aboriginals did not really know the origin of the paintings, over the years a myth had developed among them that the *Mimi* were small stick-like people who were never seen by humans, because if approached they would blow on a rock which would open and allow them to jump inside. So the *Mimi* became a useful, mystical source of inexplicable events. In the rock galleries in West Arnhem Land, groups of up to thirty *Mimi* figures may be seen engaged in battle, or hunting and are obviously the composition of one artist who has created the whole group. There is a remarkable similarity in style to the early stick figures found in Europe and Africa. Strong elements of movement and composition are evident in all of them.

4. **Central Arnhem Land**

Milingimbi, in the Crocodile Islands, only a few kilometres off shore, has long been the home of such famous artists as Djawa, Dawdi, Malangi, and Dhatanggu, to name just a few. Before white contact, Milingimbi was the meeting place for many clans where they assembled at the onset of the North West Monsoon to await the coming of the Macassan traders. Huge middens of small bi-valves three metres high and seven metres in diameter seem to indicate that large groups waited for considerable periods. Ground edge hand axes have been found in these middens and associated carbon was dated at c. 8,000 B.C. Milingimbi is the site of the famous 'Macassar Well' and many tamarind trees, around the well and along the foreshore, bear testimony to the Macassan contact.

Probably owing to the proximity of hostile people on the mainland and further west, this contact was not nearly as well developed as in North East Arnhem Land so the impact on the culture of the *Yulngor* in this area was not as significant. Although visual contact with the designs on the batik cloth led to the background in the paintings being fully cross hatched, this work may not indicate the moiety ownership of the design, as in the north east. Rather, it symbolises grassy plains, salt water, rocks or other natural elements. Many totemic symbols are represented, with the older artists painting symbolic mythology associated with the mortuary rites and initiation ceremonies of the *Gupupuynggu, Liagalawumirri, Manharrngu,* and *Wulaki* Clans.

It was Malangi's painting of the *Manharrngu* mortuary rites, with the great hunter *Gurumarringu* as the central figure, that was reproduced on the one dollar note. The *Wawilak* sisters and the serpent *Yurlungurr* dominate the *Dhuwa* ceremonies. Dawdi (now deceased) and Dhatanggu were the 'Keepers' of the secrets of these ceremonies. After Dawdi's death, because there were no young men in the *Liagalawumirri* Clan who had completed the five ceremonies to raise them to *Ngarra* rank, the designs and symbolism he favoured have completely disappeared. This circumstance has been repeated many times throughout Arnhem Land in the past ten years.

Dhatanggu, who relates the same mythology through his paintings by using the same symbols, expresses them in a completely different manner. The *Birrikili* ceremonies performed for circumcision, and mortuary rites are shown in bark paintings depicting the sacred turtles hunting shellfish in the Banyan Creek, with endless variations on this theme. In the past, paintings associated with the *Birrkulda, Bunimburr* and *Djalambu* ceremonies were produced but these have not been in evidence in recent years.

5. North East Arnhem Land

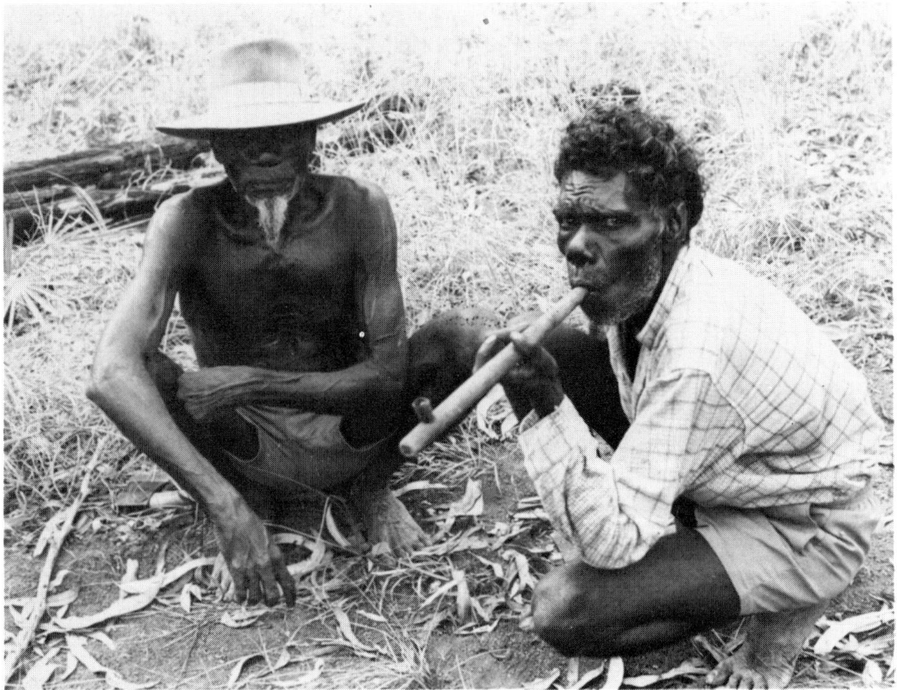

Mawalan wearing Macassan beard and Nanyin smoking Macassan pipe.

In this area the Macassan traders were completely accepted and made a deep impact on the culture. Macassan words are found in the language and it was here the *lippa lippa* (dug out canoe) with the great *tombala* (mat sail) was accepted from the Macassans and spread all through Arnhem Land and down into the Gulf. It is thought that carvings in the round originated from Macassan mortuary posts. The mortuary ceremonies of the *Yirritja* Moiety were greatly influenced by this Macassan contact so much so that one of the most important is called the Macassan prau ceremony. Old Mathaman (now deceased) when asked why this ceremony was performed said 'as the Macassans raised their sails and sailed away so the dead man's spirit has left us'. Some *Yulngor* returned with the traders to Macassar and some married Macassan women and the delicate Malay skeletal structure and light skin can be observed in this area today. The captains of the praus were greatly admired and these captains wore a short tuft of beard on the chin. This custom was adopted by the *Yulngor* as a badge of rank permitted only to the elders when they had achieved the status of 'Old Man'. To this day it is worn only by the most senior men and known as the 'Macassar beard'.

Contact is most evident in the bark paintings. So impressed were the *Yulngor* by the designs on the batik cloth brought by the traders, that they adopted them, with modifications, as background designs for their totemic symbols. These cross hatched backgrounds were given *Yulngor* significance and so passed into their mythology, becoming moiety and in some cases clan designs. The *Dhuwa* Moiety adopted straight and parallel lines with fine cross hatching in between, representing the streams of sand sent sliding down the sandhills as *Djalangbara* by *Djanda* the Sacred Goanna who startled, ran away at the approach of the *Djunkgawul*. These spirit ancestors made land fall there, after the voyage from *Baralku,* the island of the dead behind the sunrise. *Walu,* the sun, *Djunkgawul's* wife, had sent streamers of light, to show the way to *Djalangbara.*

The *Yirritja* designs by contrast consist of triangles and diamonds of different forms representing fire, clouds, running water, brakish water and rocks. Recognition of the clan designs becomes difficult when, in strict adherence to kinship law, a *Dhuwa* man has a *Yirritja* mother and this gives him the right to use certain *Yirritja* symbols in his work. The children are skin graded according to paternal lineage and when a man marries he must marry across the moiety line into another clan; his children then belong to their father's clan.

The following diagram shows the social structure of moieties and clans.

Dhuwa Moiety		**Yirritja Moiety**
Leader: Milirrpum	Equal rank	*Leader:* Mungurrawuy
Clans		Clans

Dhuwa clans	Moiety Line	Yirritja clans
Rirradjingu		*Manggalili*
Djapu		*Dalwanggu*
Kalpu		*Murunggun*
Marakulu		*Biringgal*
Naymil		*Bralbral*
Dalamiri		*Gomaidj*
Others		Others

As well as specific definitions on background designs, the moiety system embraces everything and with surprising orderliness people, flora and fauna, colours, astronomical bodies and even chants and dances are allocated to one moiety or the other.

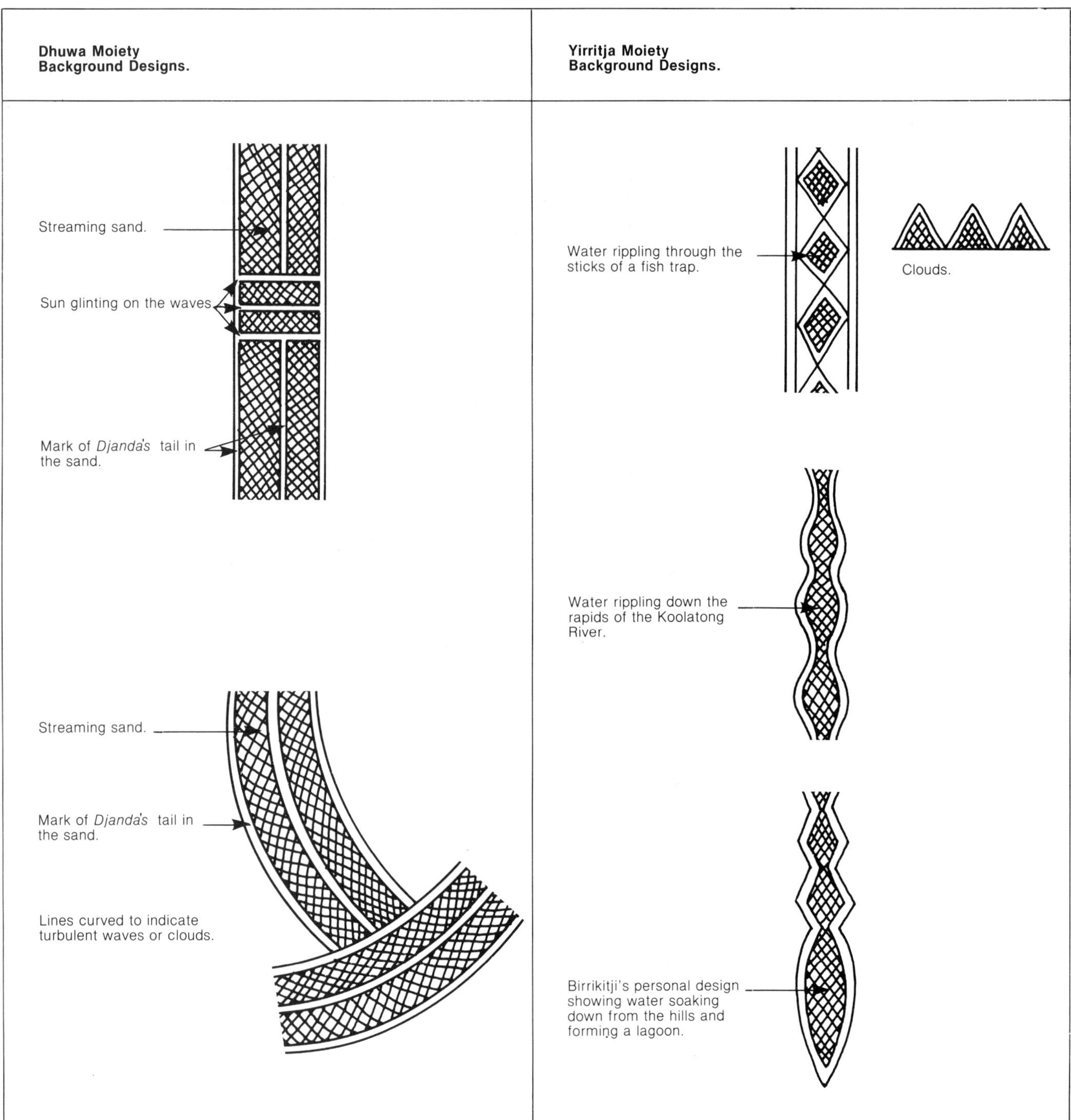

Dhuwa Moiety
Background Designs.

Yirritja Moiety
Background Designs.

Streaming sand.

Sun glinting on the waves.

Mark of Djanda's tail in
the sand.

Streaming sand.

Mark of Djanda's tail in
the sand.

Lines curved to indicate
turbulent waves or clouds.

Water rippling through the
sticks of a fish trap.

Clouds.

Water rippling down the
rapids of the Koolatong
River.

Birrikitji's personal design
showing water soaking
down from the hills and
forming a lagoon.

Narritjin Maymuru

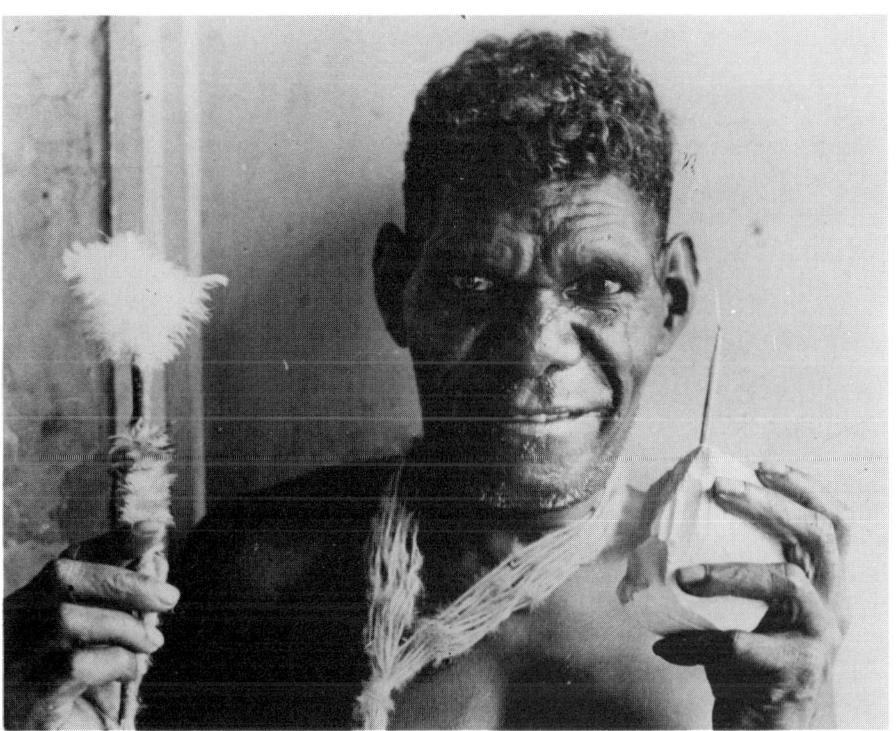

Narritjin Maymuru was born in approximately 1912 in *Manggalili* country, between Caledon Bay and Blue Mud Bay, on the western shores of the Gulf of Carpentaria. In this area he lived until his early twenties when he travelled north to Yirrkala, to the newly established mission there. Until then, he led a fully tribal life, knowing no other law than the 'old law', and hunting with his relatives using the traditional stone tipped spear and woomera. He would also have participated in whatever ceremonies were appropriate to his age grade. He was a great warrior and in 1932 was involved in the massacre of the Japanese pearlers at Caledon Bay.

He has remained intimately involved with his culture and has been a powerful force in holding the *Manggalili* Clan together in the *Yulngor* tradition. When the bauxite mining company moved into the Melville Bay area, he was most concerned about the violation of his country and, through his mission-educated son, wrote a letter of protest to Mr. Harry Guiese, Director of Aboriginal Welfare. Narritjin travelled the 500 or so miles to Darwin, living off the land and swimming crocodile and shark infested rivers, to finally hand the letter to Mr. Guiese in his office.

Today the wheel has turned full circle and Narritjin; with other members of his clan, are busily engaged in re-establishing themselves in their old 'country' at the *Manggalili* outstation at *Djarrakpi* on Cape Shield.

Manggalili Bark Paintings

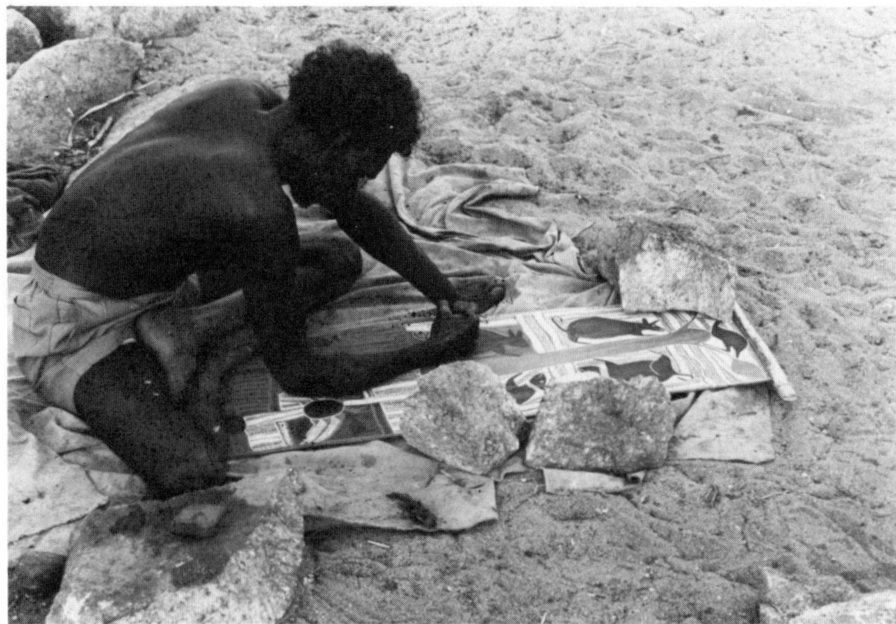

Bark paintings are significant to clan members in many different ways. As well, in the clan designs the patterns are interwoven with the ownership of chants, dances and mythology. Some are painted for the guidance of the body painters, or tell a portion of clan mythology, some are stylized maps of sacred sites whilst others are associated with mortuary rites. The designs are also regarded as permission from the supernatural world to occupy clan lands. They establish a link between the spiritual world of the ancestral beings who created the land, and the living clan members. The designs on the paintings in this exhibition are the exclusive property of the *Manggalili* Clan and Narritjin Maymuru is the 'Keeper'. His permission must be obtained before another member of the clan may create a painting and this he is entitled to do only if he has completed the requisite number of ceremonies. Even though Nanyin was Narritjin's brother, he always had to ask permission before painting a bark. Narritjin says 'the paintings are the *Manggalili* law, they tell us who we are and where we are going'.

Narritjin is very proud of the fact that the Opossum Tree myth is one of the oldest in Arnhem Land and is 'straight', his words meaning that kinship laws have been strictly observed in all clan marriages, thereby avoiding any dispute about clan ownership of designs.

On examination of the paintings it will be observed that although they are of the *Yirritja* Moiety, triangular and diamond forms are only seen in a few of them. Nor do background designs conform to the *Dhuwa* specifics. In the art of the Arnhem Landers there is always the exception to the rule, and this is one of the exceptions. The designs in these paintings show the tracks left by the Opossum, cloud patterns on the sand dunes at *Djarrakpi,* tracks left in the sand by the *Gunyan* Crab and the parallel lines of

Nanyin — Narritjin's brother — with Macassan pipe contemplating his work.

foam left on the beach by the receding tide. These paintings are portions of the Opossum Tree mythology.

In the days of the beginning, *Banaitja* and *Barama,* with other supernatural beings, came out of the sea and the sea foam dried on their bodies and formed a diamond patterned grid. This diamond pattern they gave to the *Yirritja* Clans. They summoned the wise man *Guwark* and gave him the power to use the wings and form of a bird, to travel about the country with the spirit woman *Ngapililingu* to carry out the work of making the sacred places and teaching the *Yulngor* the correct customs.

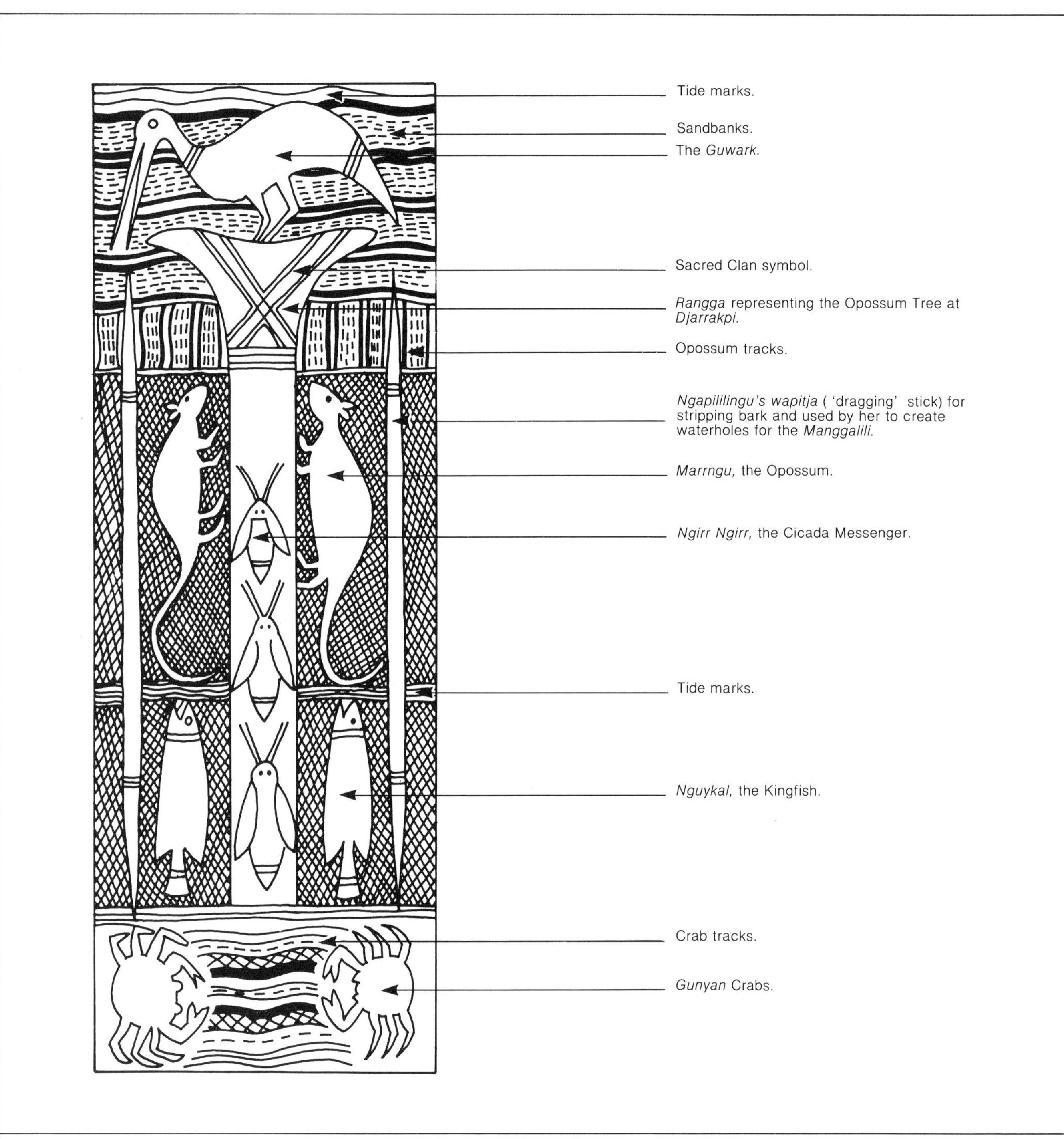

Tide marks.
Sandbanks.
The Guwark.
Sacred Clan symbol.
Rangga representing the Opossum Tree at Djarrakpi.
Opossum tracks.
Ngapililingu's wapitja ('dragging' stick) for stripping bark and used by her to create waterholes for the Manggalili.
Marrngu, the Opossum.
Ngirr Ngirr, the Cicada Messenger.
Tide marks.
Nguykal, the Kingfish.
Crab tracks.
Gunyan Crabs.

The Opossum Tree Myth

In the 'Dreaming', the night bird *Guwark* became lonely and set out to find his friend *Marrngu,* the Opossum, to talk to. During the day he found him at several places but *Marrngu* would not talk to him because it was daylight. Ever since, the *Guwark* only calls at night as he knows this is the only time *Marrngu* will answer him. During his travels that day, as he flew along the coast, he saw the Kingfish, *Nguykal* and, feeling hungry, he called out *'Nguykal* if you will jump out of the water on to the sand I will give you some land'. *Nguykal* did so and was gobbled up by the *Guwark.* At long last he came to *Djarrakpi* and in the moonlight he saw the sacred tree on the cliff. As he was very tired, it was with great relief that he landed in the top of the tree and noticed the *Gunyan* Crabs playing in the sand at the foot of the cliff, running from their holes through the parallel lines of foam left by the ebbing tide. As he sat looking about, he heard a noise and realized *Marrngu* was inside the hollow tree. He then sent *Ngirr Ngirr,* the Cicada, down the tree with a message to *Marrngu* who came up the tree to the *Guwark* and they spent the night talking about the sacred places of the *Manggalili.* They then sent *Ngirr Ngirr* with a message to *Ngapililingu* and asked her to come with them into the *Manggalili* country. The Opossum travelled ahead and left a path for them to follow. Before the *Guwark* and *Ngapililingu* came together at *Djarrakpi,* when they met at the sacred Opossum Tree (*Gayawu,* the Wild Cashew Tree) *Guwark* had already travelled extensively with *Ngirr Ngirr* his messenger, and named sacred places for the *Manggalili. Ngapililingu* is a somewhat mystical being hovering in the background of the mythology; information about her is very sparingly given and only after many years of contact. She taught the *Yulngor* women many things; how to make the paper bark water carrier, how to look for the bulb 'yoko' and prepare it for eating, how to make bark string and weave pandanus palm baskets. She came to the mainland from Groote Eylandt, travelling in a giant sized, bark water container with a band of specially trained spirit women known as the *Warruthilaku,* who eventually split up to become the different language and clan groups of the *Yirritja* Moiety, including the *Manggalili.* A more important part of *Ngapililingu's* work was naming flora and fauna and making them *Yirritja* totems, naming sacred places and making *mariian.* The 'dragging' stick (*wapitja*) which she made for stripping bark, is a very important symbol on the bark paintings as with this she made all the *Yirritja* water holes.

James Davidson
Collector of Aboriginal
and Oceanic Art.

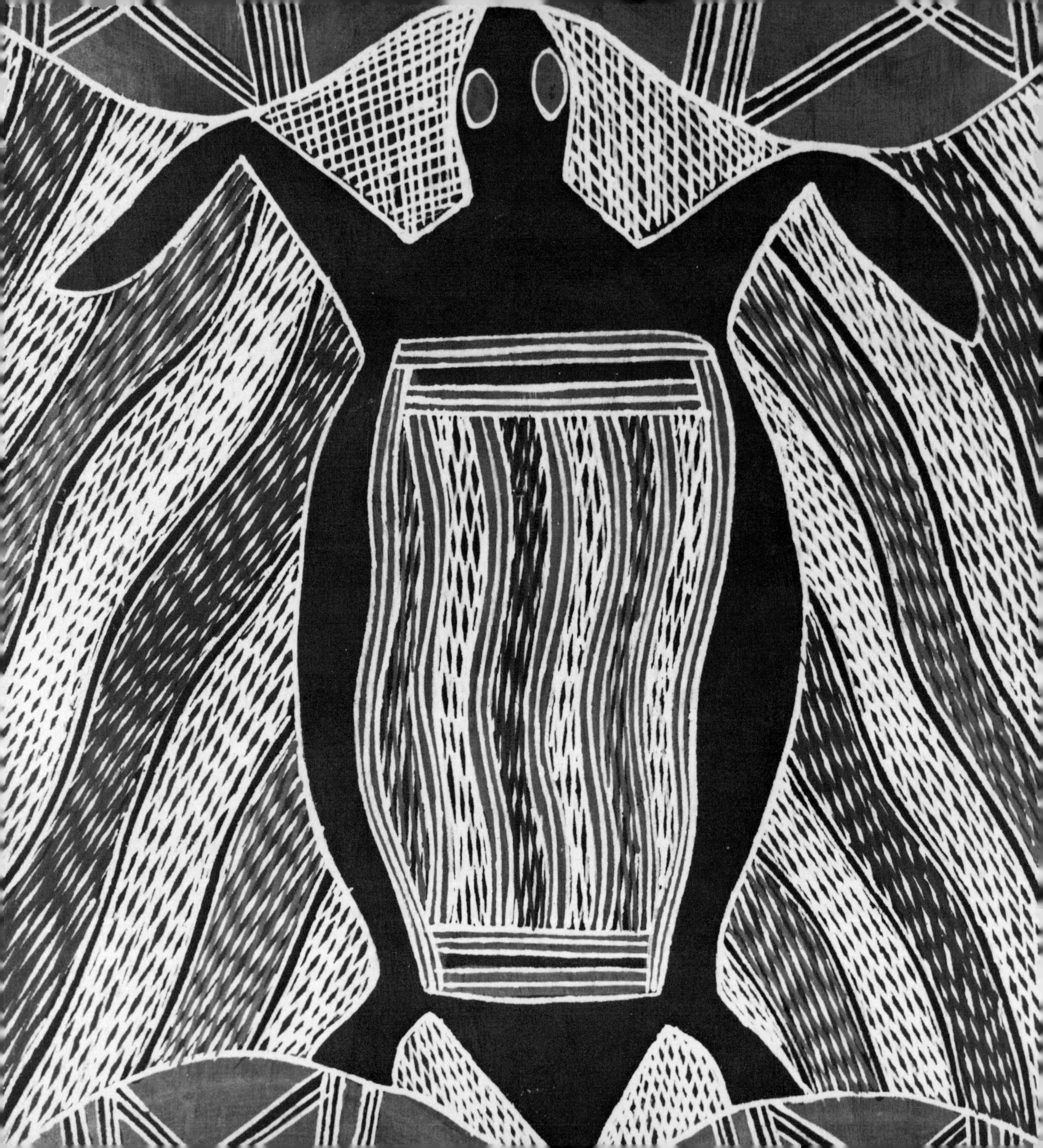

Description of Manggalili Bark Paintings and Artefacts

1. **The Gunyan Crab in Djarrakpi Landscape**

Narritjin Maymuru born 1922
Yirritja Moiety, Manggalili Clan
Djarrakpi, N.E. Arnhem Land
Ochre on bark
110 x 50 cm
Collection: Mr. James Davidson

The central symbol in this painting is the *Gunyan* Crab who was playing with his brothers on the sand at the foot of the cliff at *Djarrakpi,* when the *Guwark* was talking with *Marrngu* about the sacred places of the *Manggalili.* The tracks left by *Marrngu* for the *Guwark* to follow are shown on the crab's body by bars of short, parallel, polychrome dashes. The double lines on the cross hatched background are the parallel lines of foam left on the beach by the receding tide. These symbols are important clan designs and are repeated as a background in the painting. Because of his importance *Marrngu* is shown twice in each of the three panels.

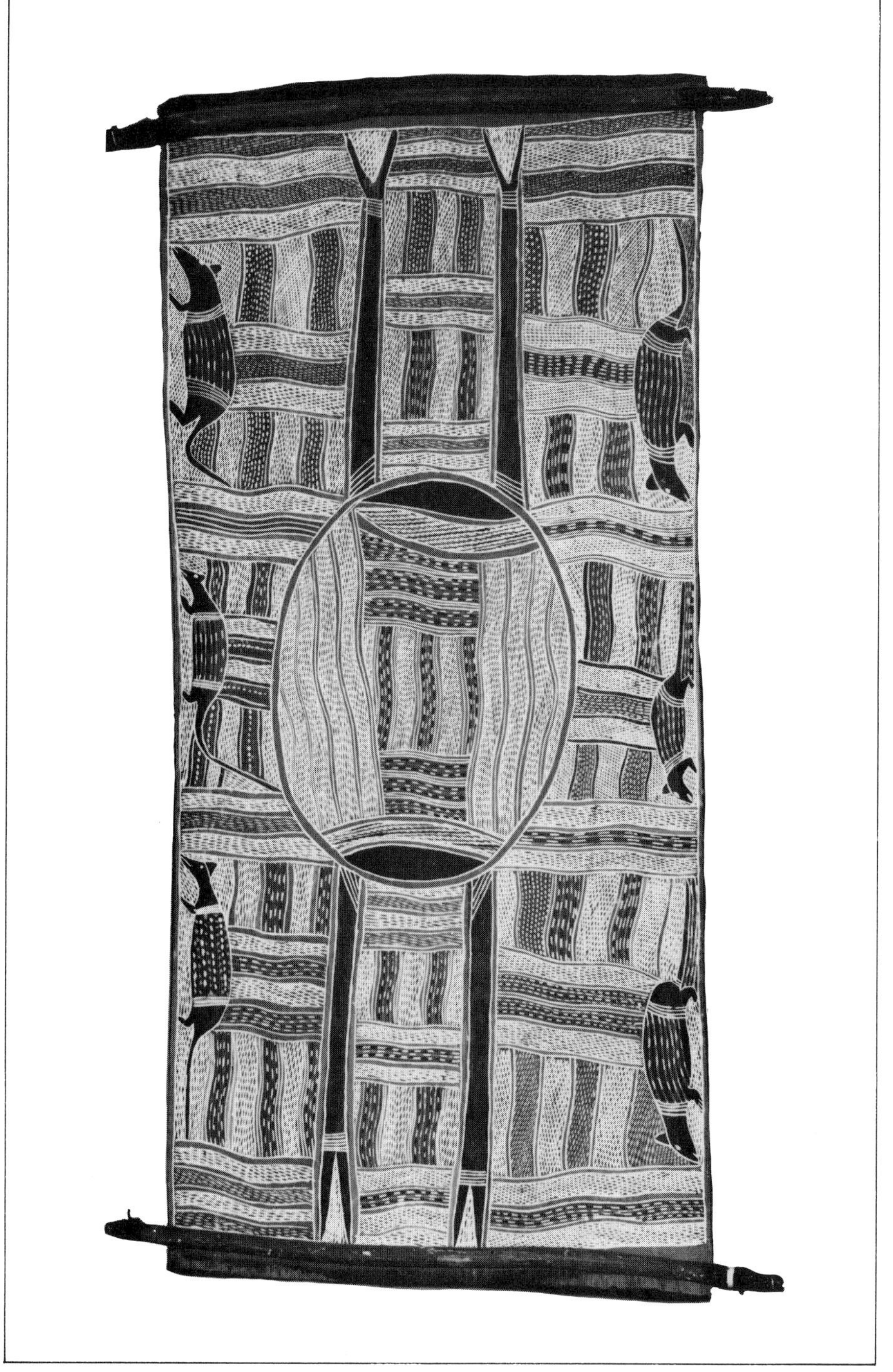

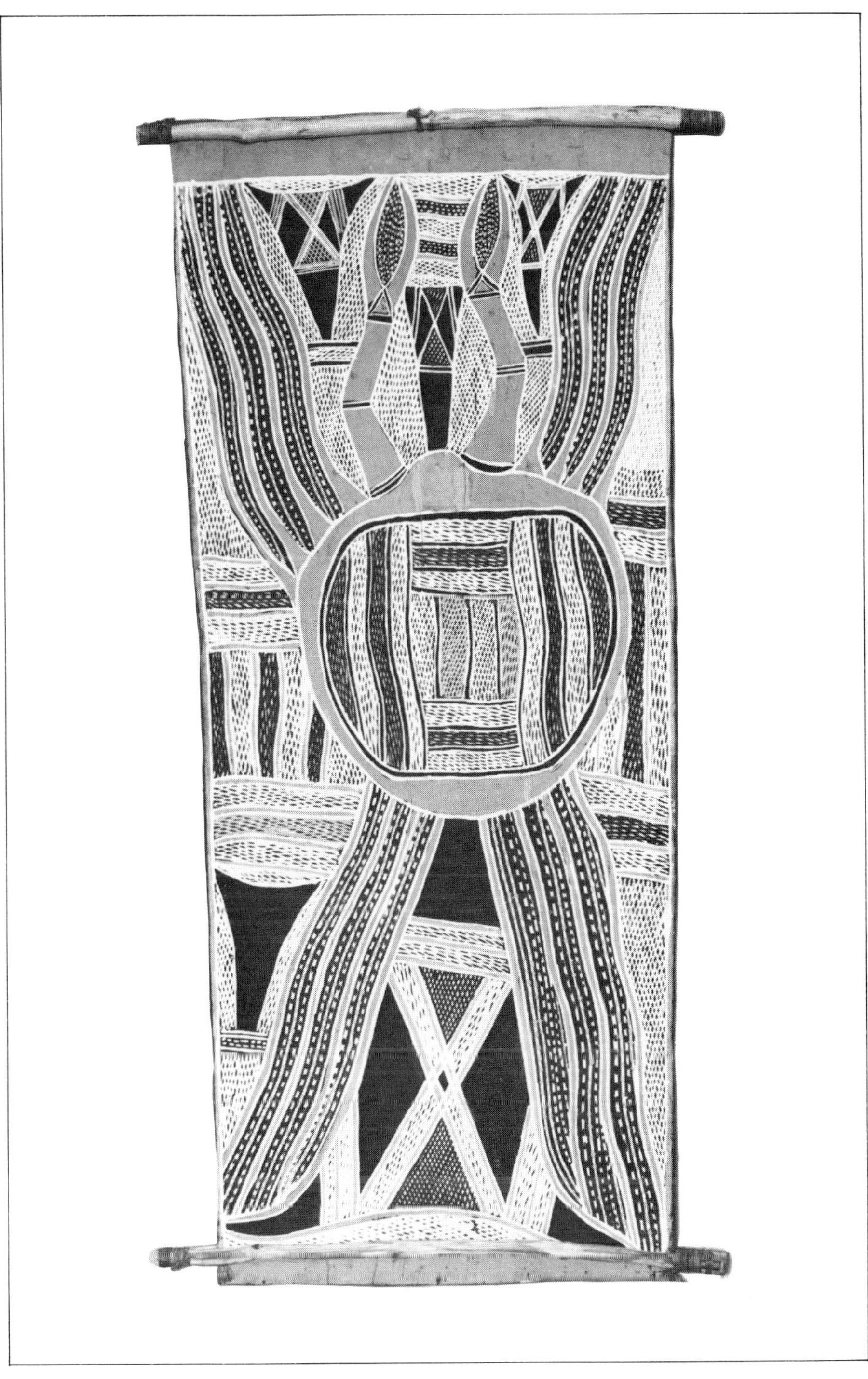

2. **The Gunyan Crab at Sacred Waterhole**

Narritjin Maymuru
Yirritja Moiety, Manggalili Clan
Djarrakpi, N.E. Arnhem Land
Ochre on bark
88 x 36 cm
Collection: Mr. James Davidson

3. **The Gunyan Crab**

Narritjin Maymuru
Yirritja Moiety, Manggalili Clan
Djarrakpi, N.E. Arnhem Land
Ochre on bark
53 x 26 cm
Collection: Mr. James Davidson

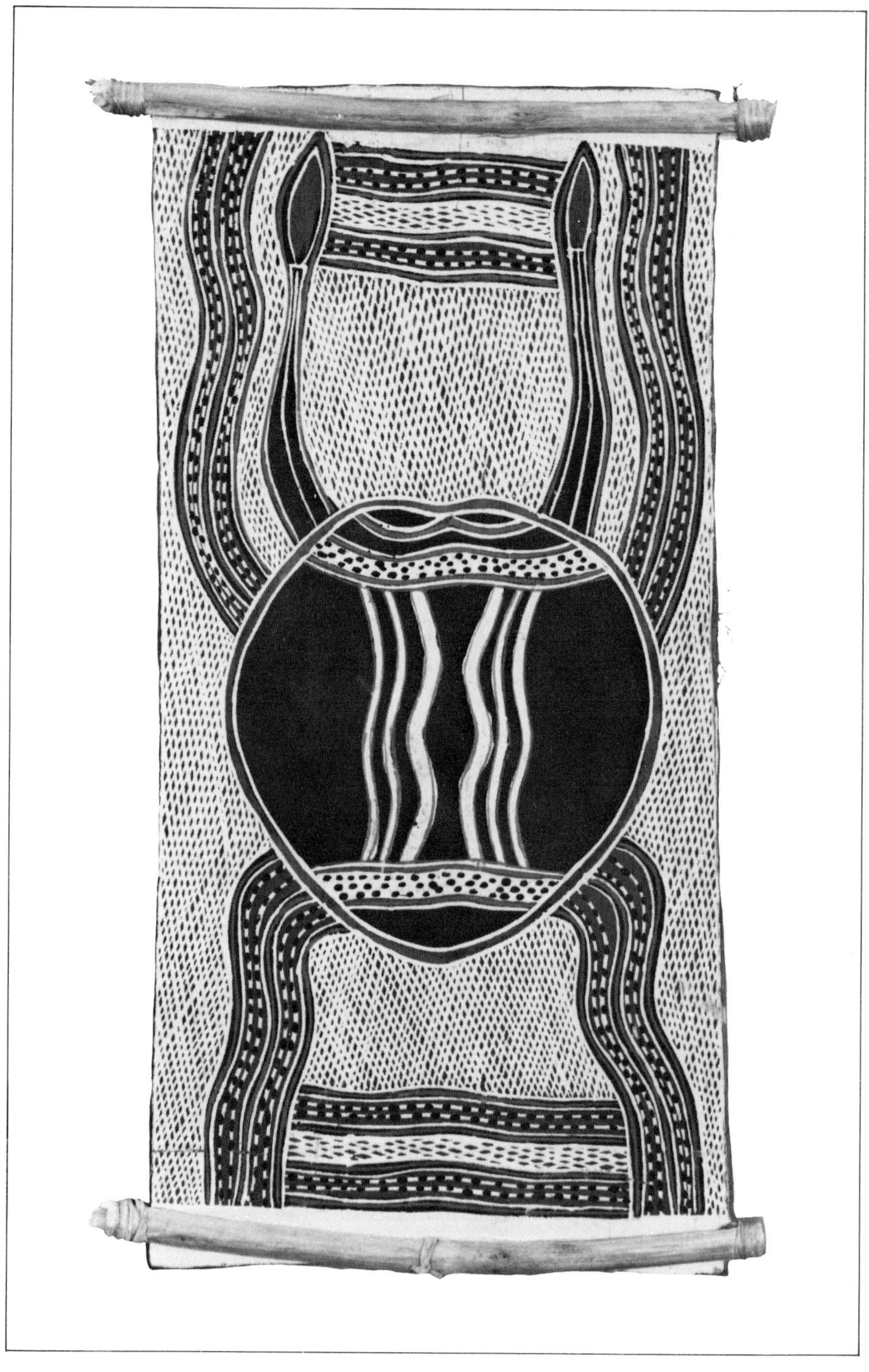

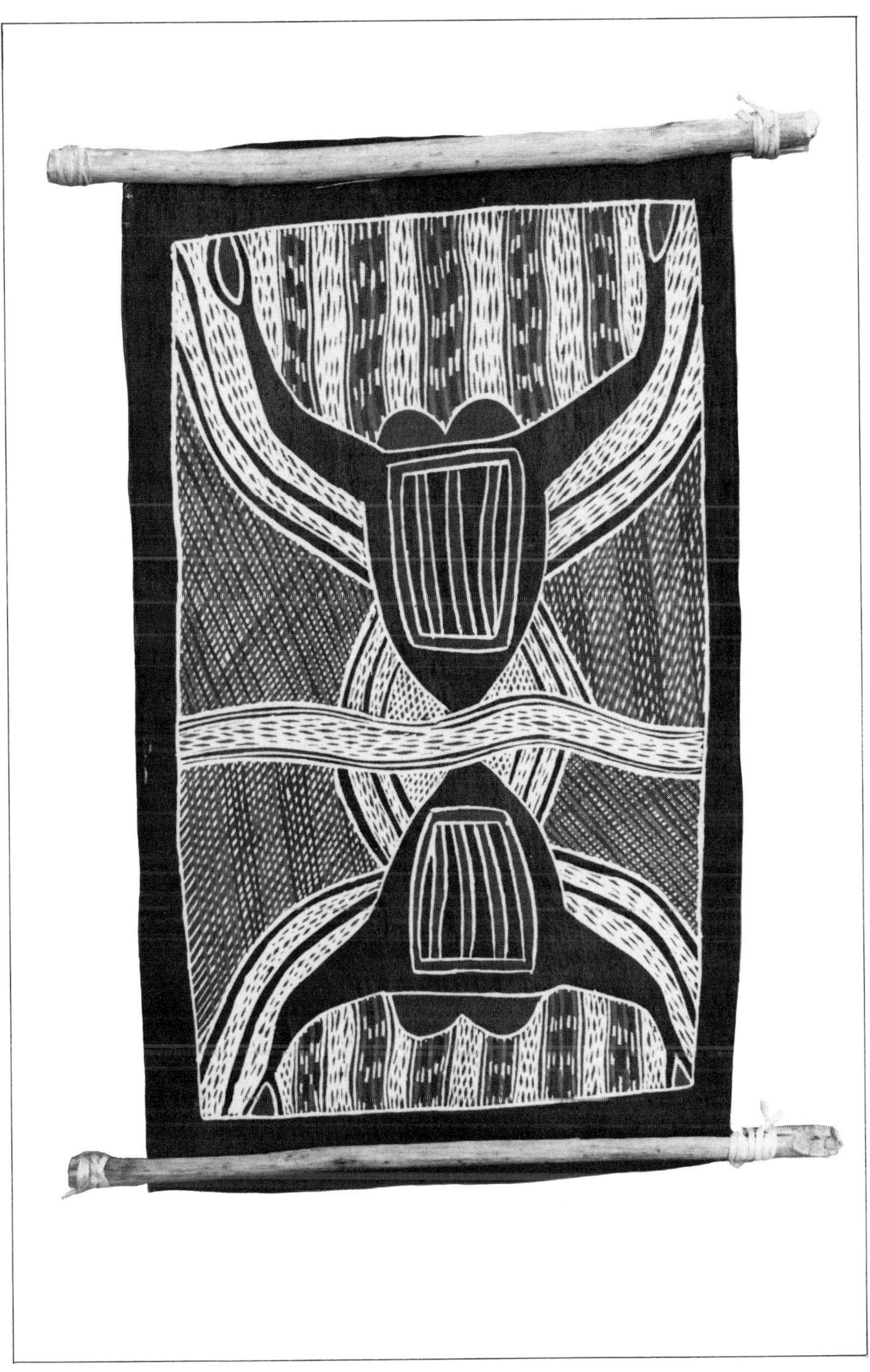

4. **The Gunyan Crab**

Narritjin Maymuru
Yirritja Moiety, Manggalili Clan
Djarrakpi, N.E. Arnhem Land
Ochre on bark
43 x 25 cm
Collection: Mr. James Davidson

5. **The Gunyan Crab with Crab Holes**

Narritjin Maymuru
Yirritja Moiety, Manggalili Clan
Djarrakpi, N.E. Arnhem Land
Ochre on bark
45 x 19 cm
Collection: Mr. James Davidson

Nos. 2, 3, 4, and 5 all refer to the same subject with additional symbols as in No. 5 where the black shapes in each represent crab holes. In No. 2 at the bottom of the painting is a most important symbol with a number of meanings. It consists of a cross which forms the *Yirritja* triangles and is also seen in three positions at the top of the painting. The small black symbol in the centre of the cross at the bottom is a sacred waterhole. Bars of cross hatching represent sand dunes created by *Ngapililingu,* the Ancestral Spirit Woman. In this group of paintings, the parallel lines, consisting of short dashes emerging from the crab's body to form legs, are also crab tracks left in the sand and are often in sacred body painting on ceremonial occasions. The crab track designs and colours were created 'in the Time before Morning' by the spirit men *Munderrwuthan* and *Ngguruguyamirri.*

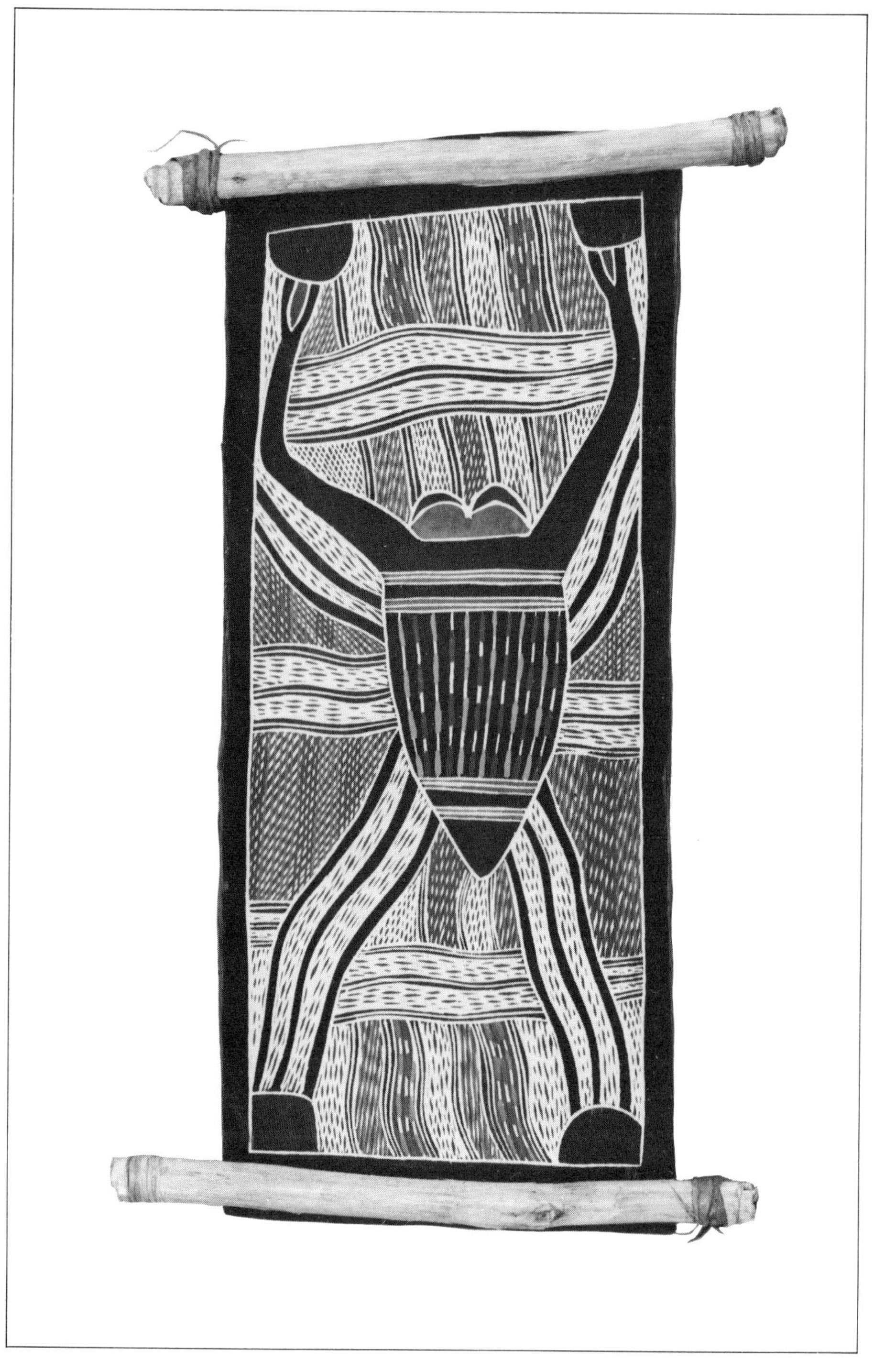

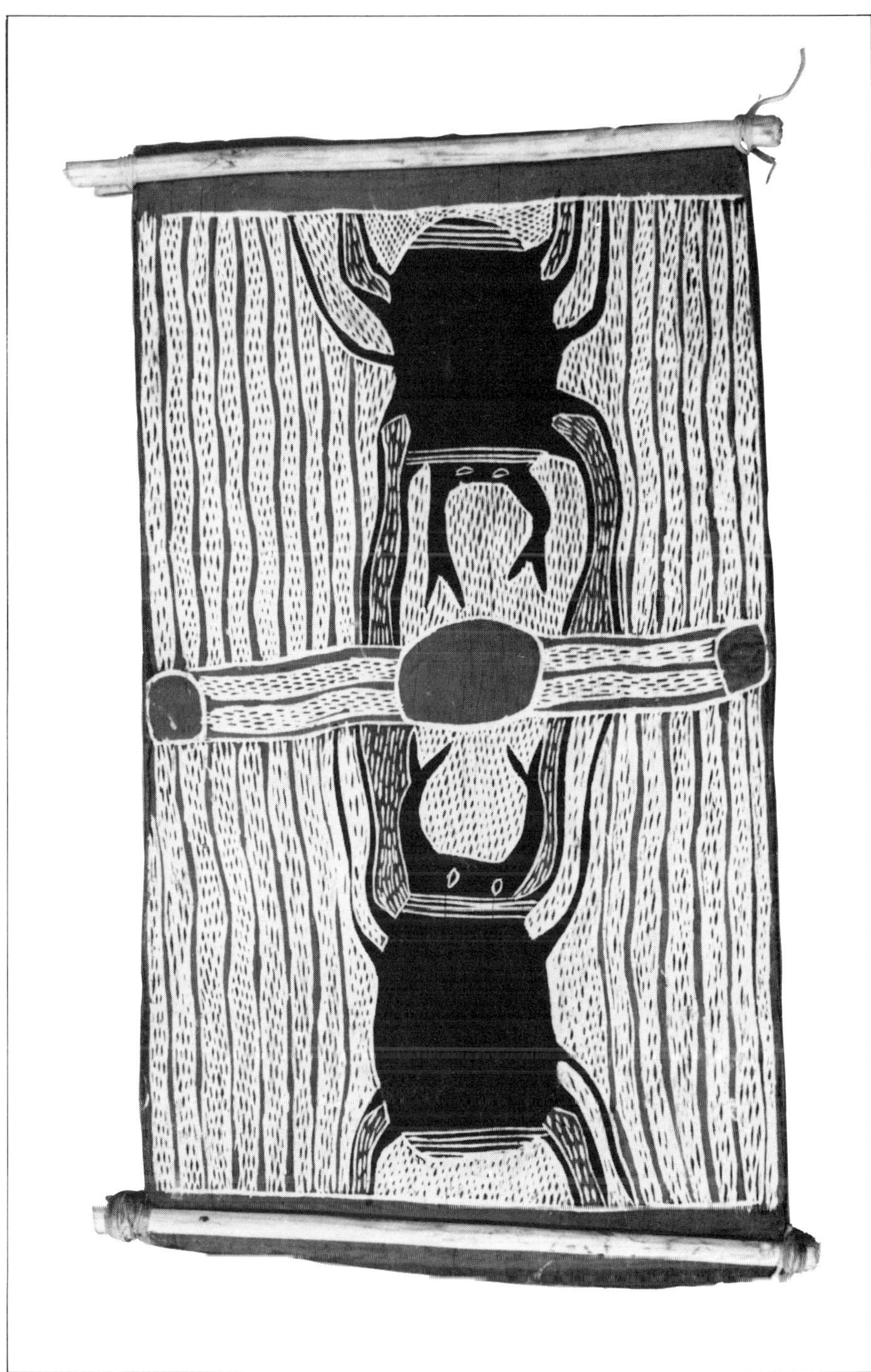

6. Gunyan Crabs against Sand Dunes

Nanyin Maymuru
Yirritja Moiety, Manggalili Clan
Djarrakpi, N.E. Arnhem Land
Ochre on bark
50 x 28 cm
Collection: Mr. James Davidson

Although Nanyin was Narritjin's elder brother, he was not the 'Keeper' for *Manggalili* mythology and every time he wanted to produce a bark painting he had to ask Narritjin's permission. As a young man, he was severely wounded high in the left breast, when he was hit by a shovel nose spear in a fight. He died in 1969. Nanyin's painting shows the *Gunyan* Crabs with the tidal foam lines and the crab track designs extending from the crab's body. The three circular symbols are crab holes. White cross hatching behind the crabs represents sand dunes.

7. **Gunyan Crabs**

Banapana Maymuru
Yirritja Moiety, Manggalili Clan
Djarrakpi, N.E. Arnhem Land
Ochre on bark
57 x 22 cm
Collection: Mr. James Davidson

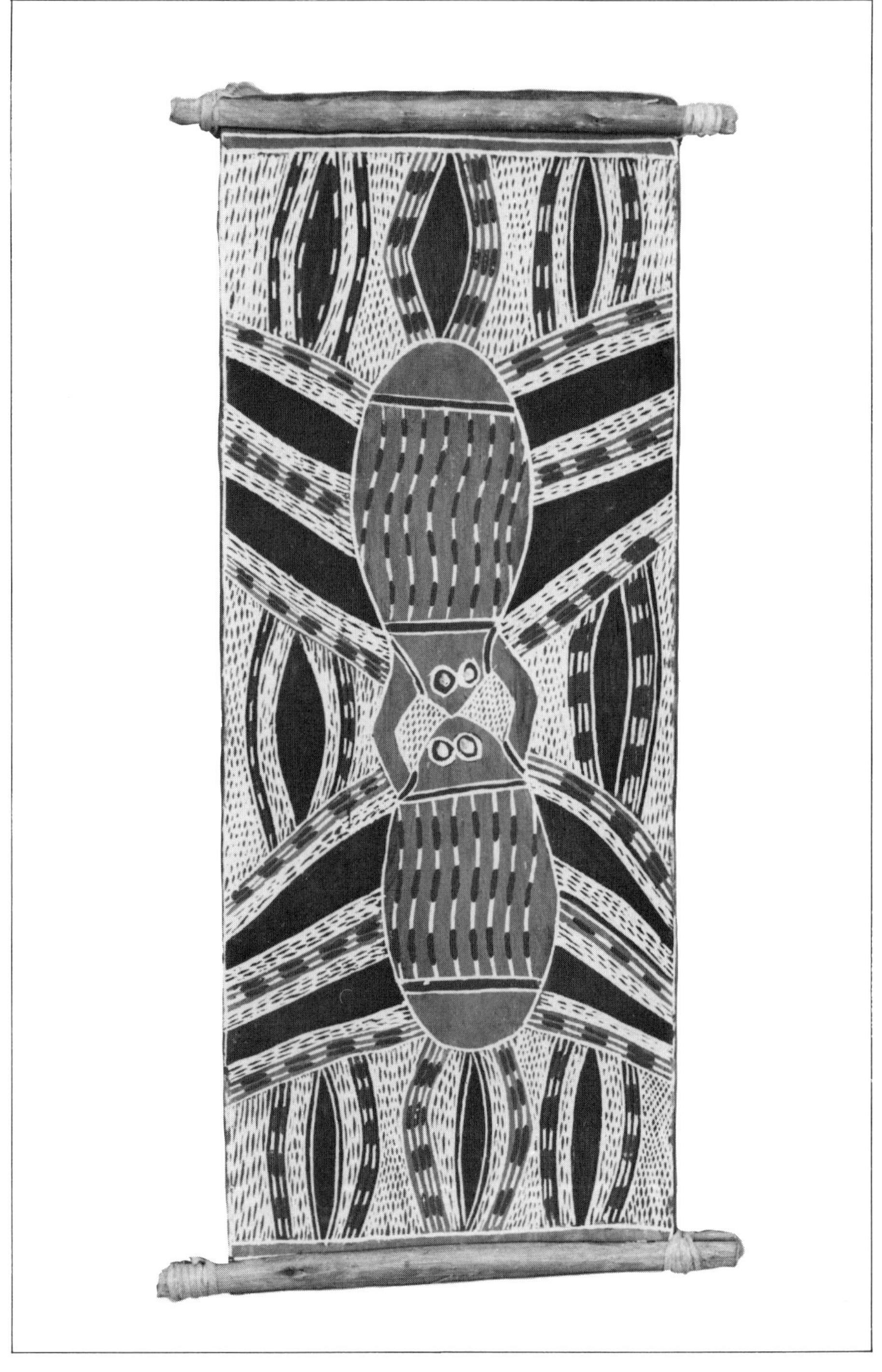

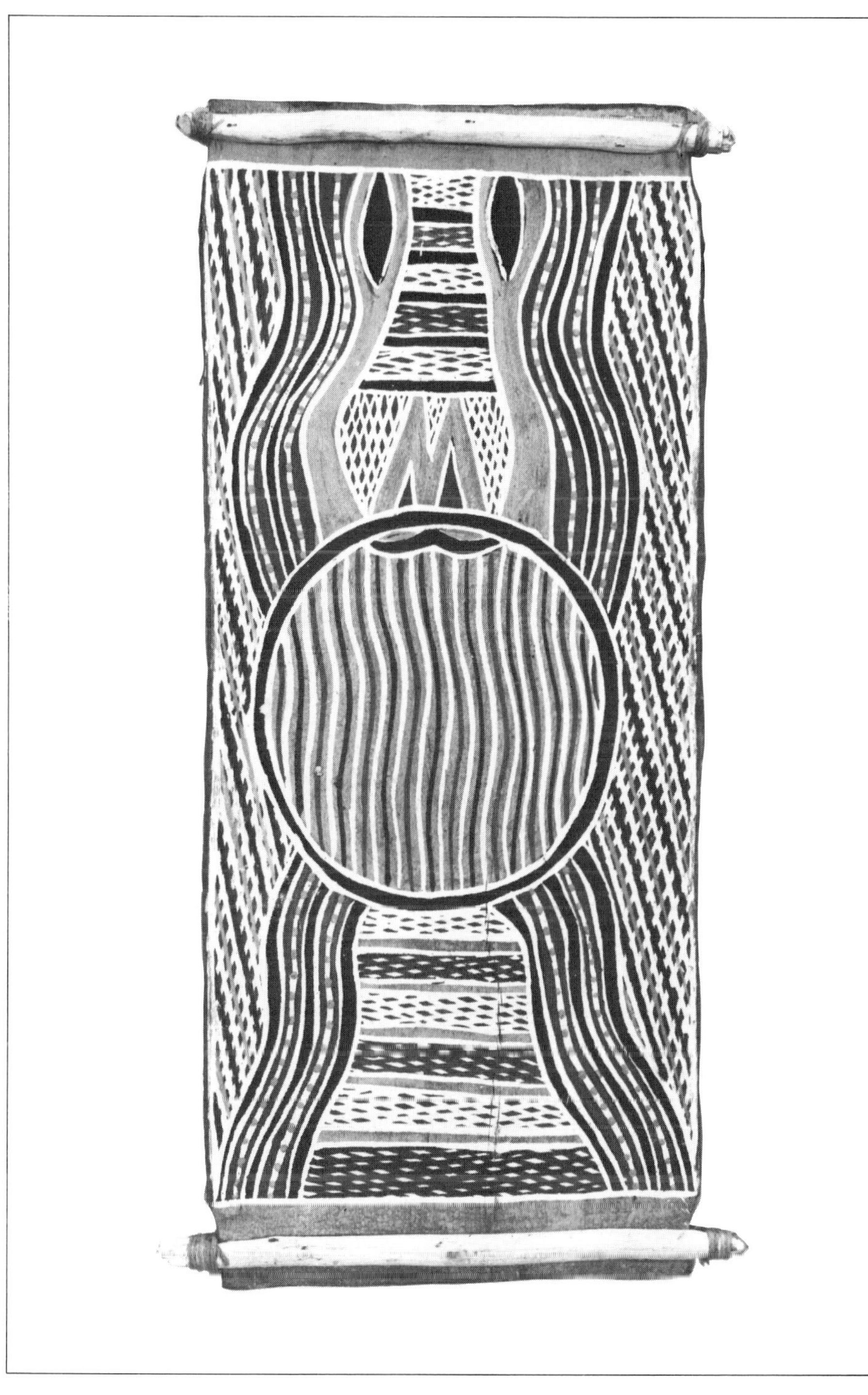

8. **Gunyan Crabs**

Banapana Maymuru
Yirritja Moiety, Manggalili Clan
Djarrakpi, N.E. Arnhem Land
Ochre on bark
42 x 18 cm
Collection: Mr. James Davidson

Banapana is Narritjin's son, and the two paintings depict the totemic *Gunyan* Crabs. As a group the paintings No. 1 to 8 painted by three different artists illustrate the remarkable variations the *Yulngor* artist may achieve in spite of having to paint within very strict limits and with only four colours. An art critic once referred to 'the tired old designs of the bark paintings of Yirrkala'. Although trained to appreciate art in the European style he was not perceptive enough to recognise the subtle differences in the work of a particular artist who had 'done his five ceremonies' to become a *Nggara* man and thus earn the right to use that particular design.

9. Ceremonial Woomeras

Narritjin Maymuru
Yirritja Moiety, Manggalili Clan
Djarrakpi, N.E. Arnhem Land
Ochre on bark
47 x 19 cm
Collection: Mr. James Davidson

This painting has a special meaning for Narritjin; as the word Narritjin in the *Manggalili* language means woomera, painting the image of a woomera is the nearest he could get to signing his name. These are two ceremonial woomeras. The hook at the top that fits into the hollow end of the spear represents the head of the *Guwark,* and the *Yirritja* totemic triangles are formed by the crossed lines of the sacred *Manggalili* symbol. On either side of the woomeras, are the two fighting spears brought from Groote Eylandt by the two spirit men *Munderrwuthan* and *Ngguruguyamirri* in the 'Dreaming'. The cross hatched background represents cloud shadows swiftly travelling across the dand dunes at *Djarrakpi* on the high winds of the North West Monsoon.

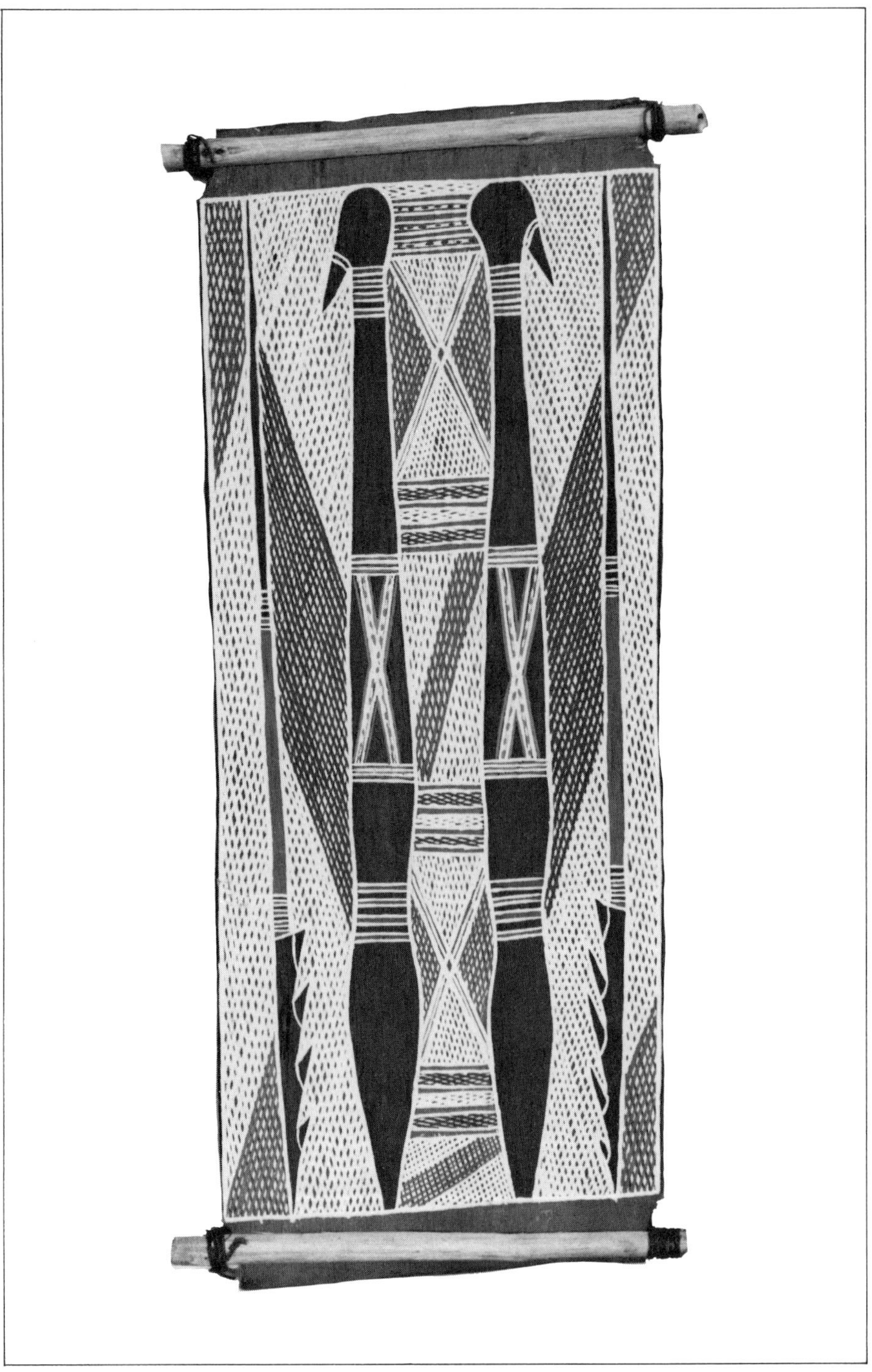

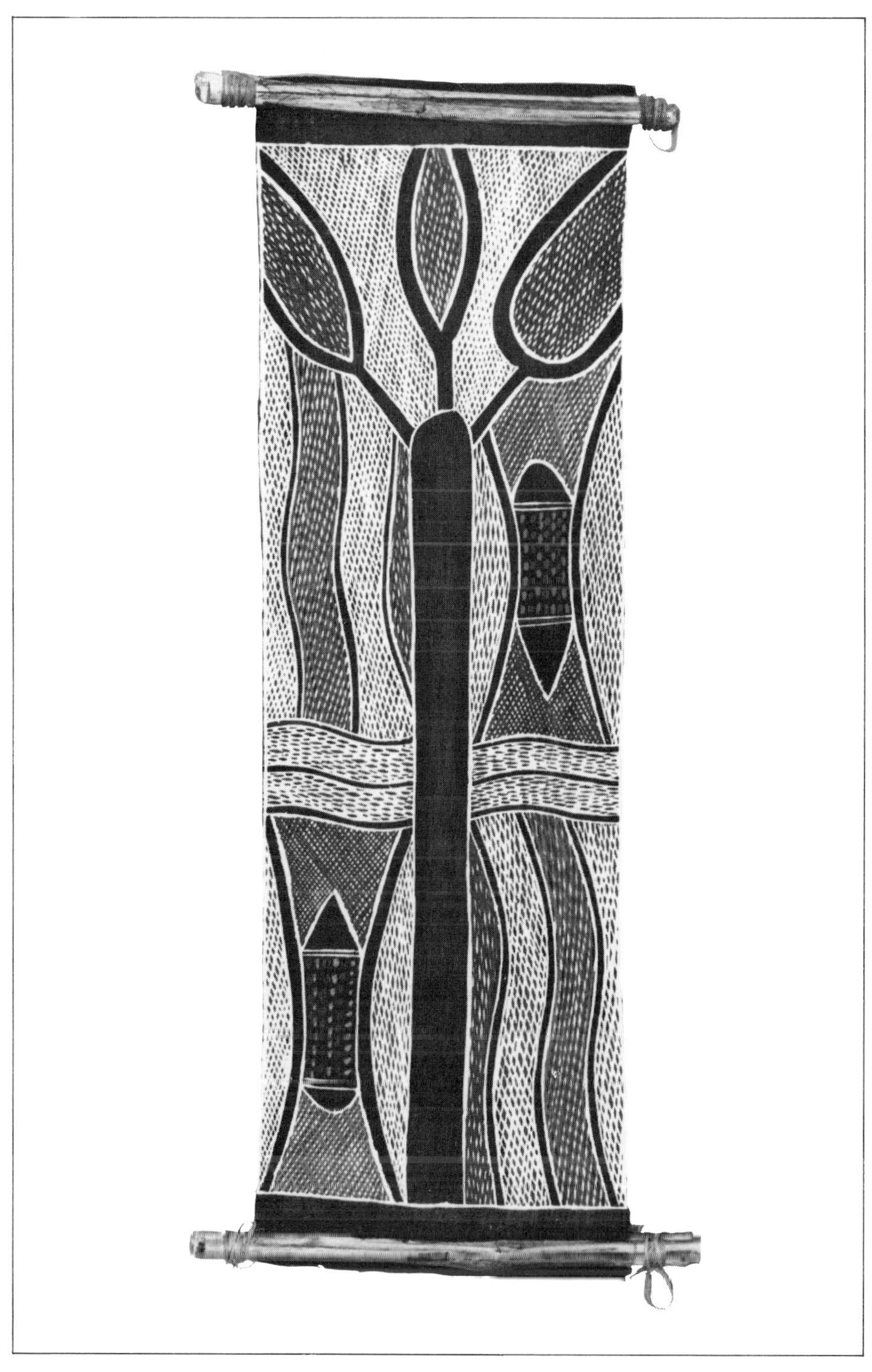

10. **Ngirr Ngirr, the Cicada Messenger**
Narritjin Maymuru
Yirritja Moiety, Manggalili Clan
Djarrakpi, N.E. Arnhem Land
Ochre on bark
51 x 16 cm
Collection: Mr. James Davidson

The central symbol is a *rangga* representing the Opossum Tree, and on either side is *Ngirr Ngirr,* the Cicada Messenger. The hatched background represents sand dunes.

11. **Marrngu, the Opossum**

Narritjin Maymuru
Yirritja Moiety, Manggalili Clan
Djarrakpi, N.E. Arnhem Land
Ochre on bark
68 x 29 cm
Collection: Mr. James Davidson

This painting shows *Marrngu,* who
because of his importance is shown
twice. The symbol in the centre has
many meanings; it is a *rangga*
representing the Opossum Tree,
because of the bird's head it is the
Guwark, and it also depicts the long
narrow sand dune on the west bank
of the lake at *Djarrakpi* which was
formed by the *Guwark* when he laid
out a long string of opossum fur.
Opossum tracks and sand dunes form
the background.

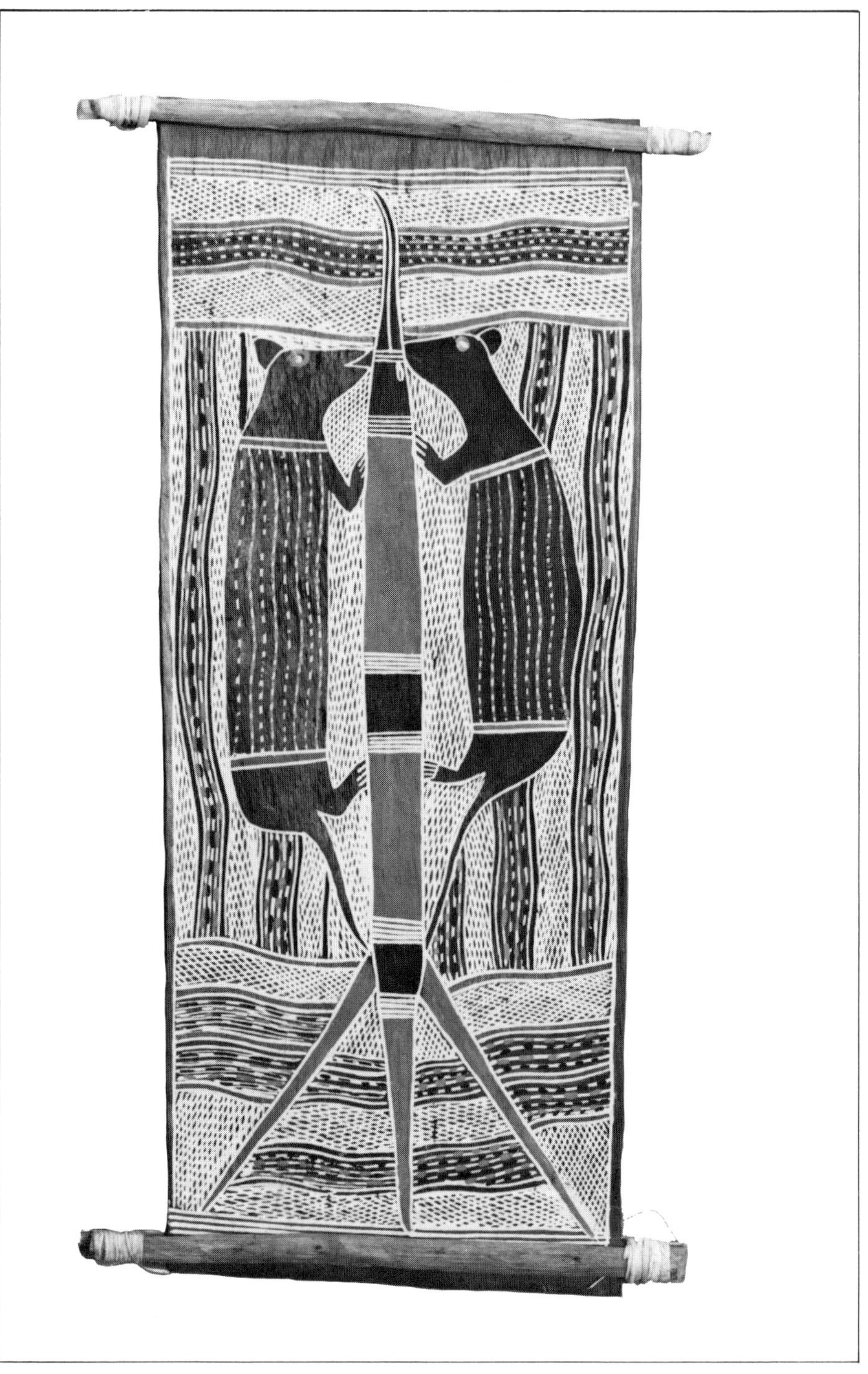

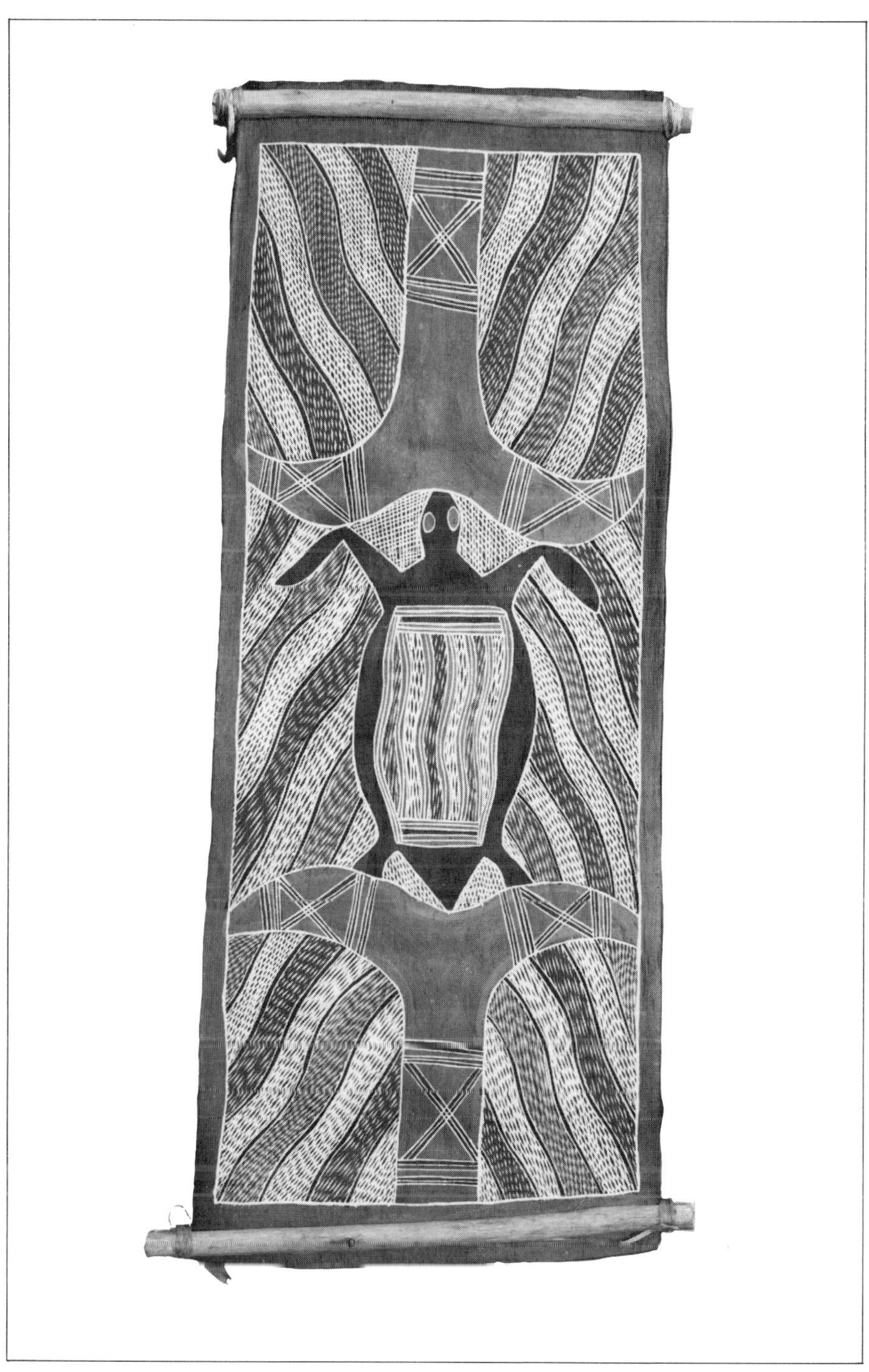

12. **Yinipunga, the Sacred Totemic Turtle**

Narritjin Maymuru
Yirritja Moiety, Manggalili Clan
Djarrakpi, N.E. Arnhem Land
Ochre on bark
77 x 27 cm
Collection: Mr. James Davidson

The two symbols at the top and bottom of the painting are the thunder heads that form over *Djarrakpi* during the North West Monsoon. This is a significant *Manggalili* symbol and for important ceremonies is painted on the bodies of the *Nggara,* or fully initiated, men thus;
On each of the thunder heads the crossed totemic lines are shown and the flowing background indicates the movement of the sea. The sacred totemic turtle *Yinipunga* is shown in the centre.

13. **Guwark, the Night Bird**

Narritjin Maymuru
Yirritja Moiety, Manggalili Clan
Djarrakpi, N.E. Arnhem Land
Ochre on bark
63 x 26 cm
Collection: Mr. James Davidson

This unusual painting shows the
Guwark in a very stylized manner.
Winding lines of dots and dashes are
Opossum tracks and outline the
Yirritja diamond forms which depict
the edible bulb 'yoko'. *Marrngu,* the
Opossum, and the Messenger, *Ngirr
Ngirr* are shown on a hatched
background depicting sand dunes and
tide marks on the beach.

14. **Marrngu, the Opossum against Background Sand Hills and Tide Marks**

Narritjin Maymuru
Yirritja Moiety, Manggalili Clan
Djarrakpi, N.E. Arnhem Land
Ochre on bark
58 x 22 cm
Collection: Mr. James Davidson

15. **Nguykal, the Kingfish**

Narritjin Maymuru
Yirritja Moiety, Manggalili Clan
Djarrakpi, N.E. Arnhem Land
Ochre on bark
57 x 18 cm
Collection: Mr. James Davidson

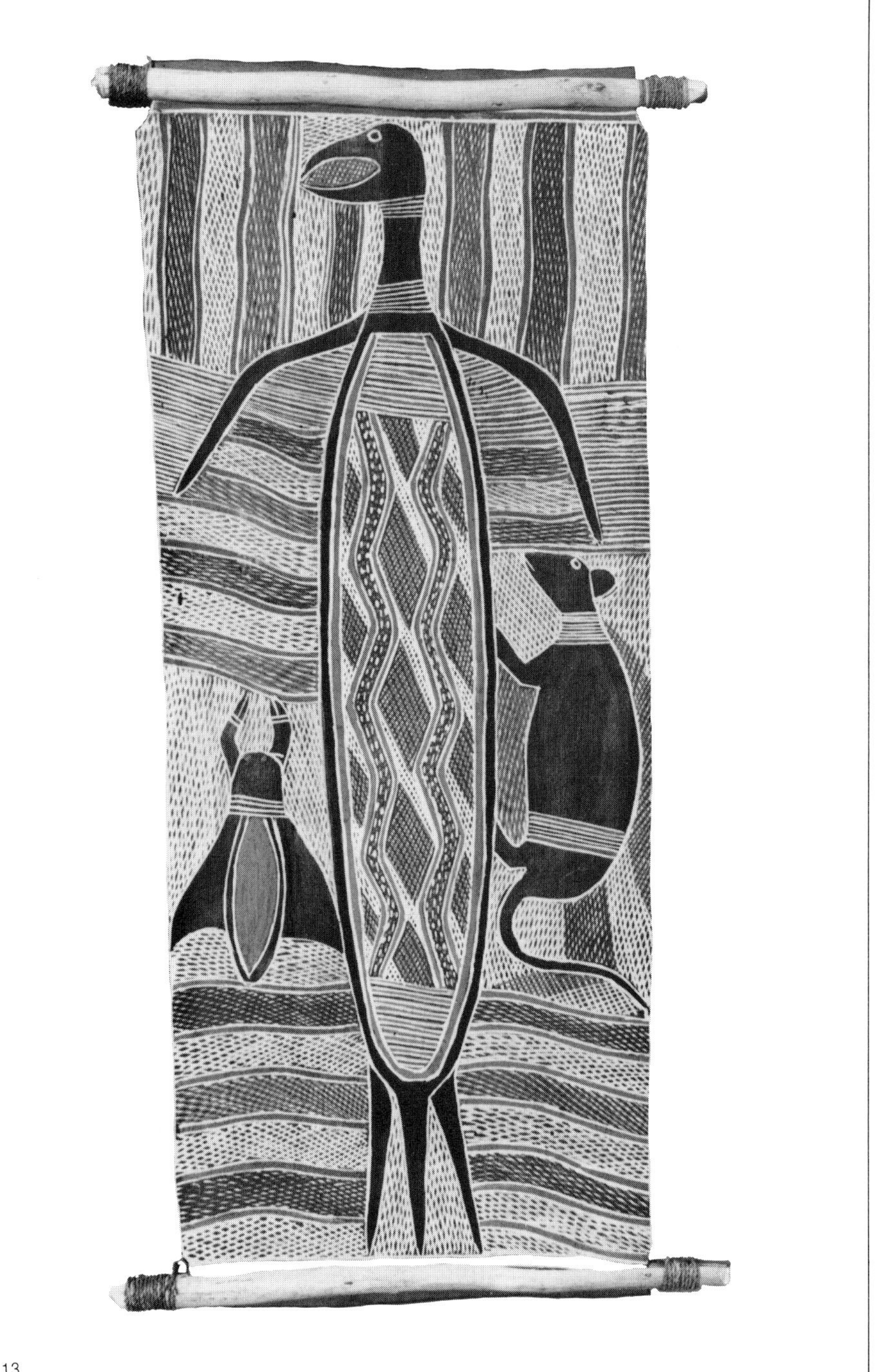

13

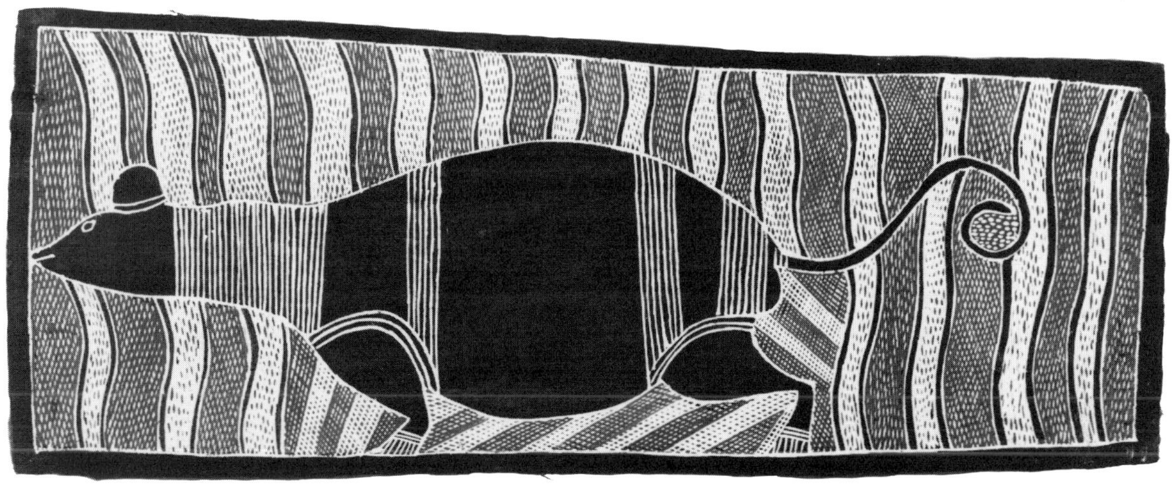

14

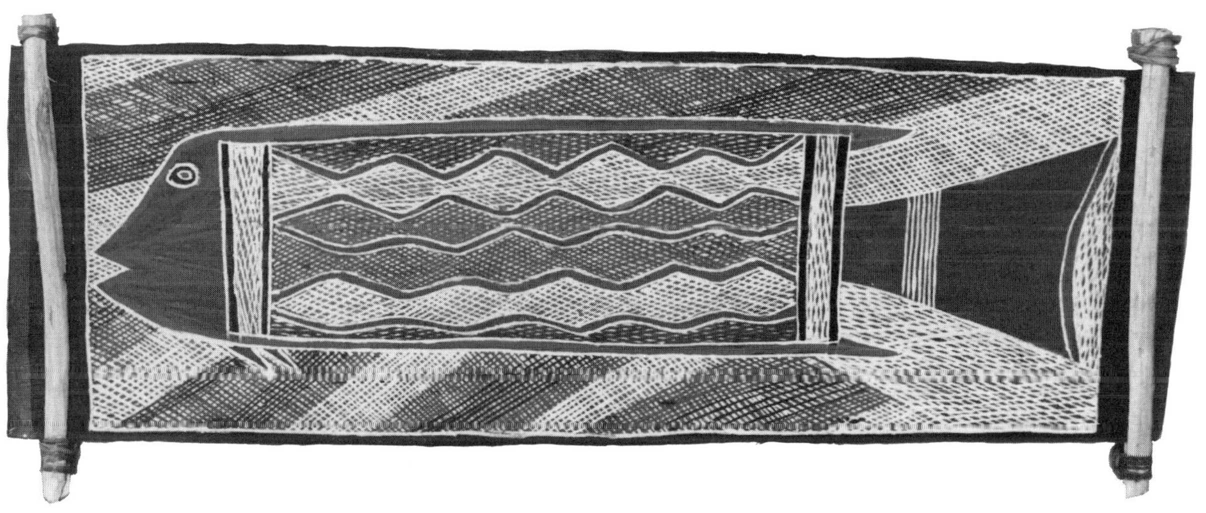

15

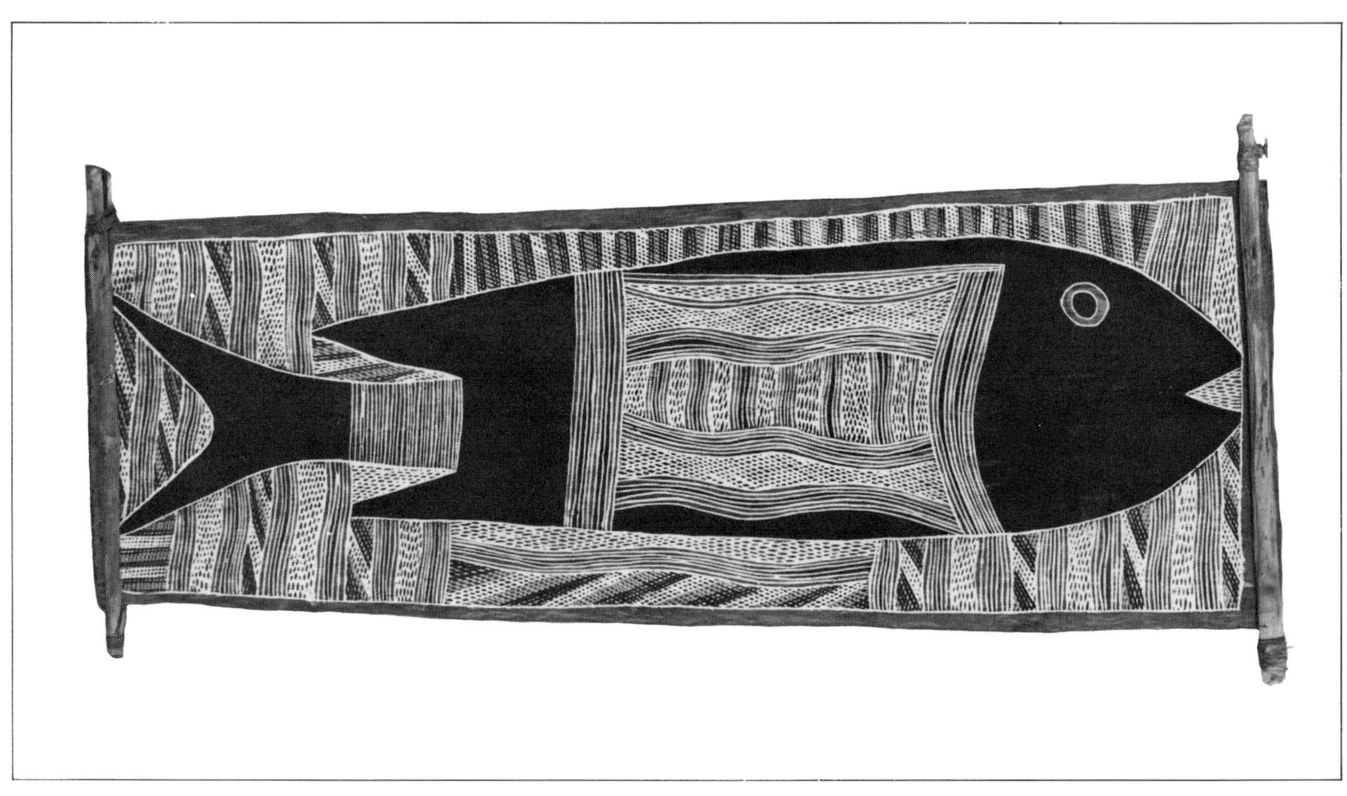

16. **Nguykal**

Narritjin Maymuru
Yirritja Moiety, Manggalili Clan
Djarrakpi, N.E. Arnhem Land
Ochre on bark
77 x 27 cm
Collection: Mr. James Davidson

Nos. 15 and 16 both show *Nguykal* the Kingfish, an important *Manggalili* totem. When the *Guwark* was searching for *Marrngu* he saw *Nguykal* and called to him and said 'jump out of the water on to the beach and I will give you some land'. *Nguykal* jumped out of the water and as soon as he was on the beach, the *Guwark* ate him. The rectangular shape of *Nguykal* in No. 15 means that a picture of the *rangga* has been painted and not the fish itself. On the body of the *rangga* is the ancient *Yirritja* design of the edible 'yoko' bulb. The background represents sandhills and seashores. No. 16 shows *Nguykal,* the Fish, as distinct from *Nguykal,* the Kingfish *rangga*. The polychrome bars of cross hatching are the reefs where *Nguykal* is to be found and the bands of parallel lines are tide marks on the beach.

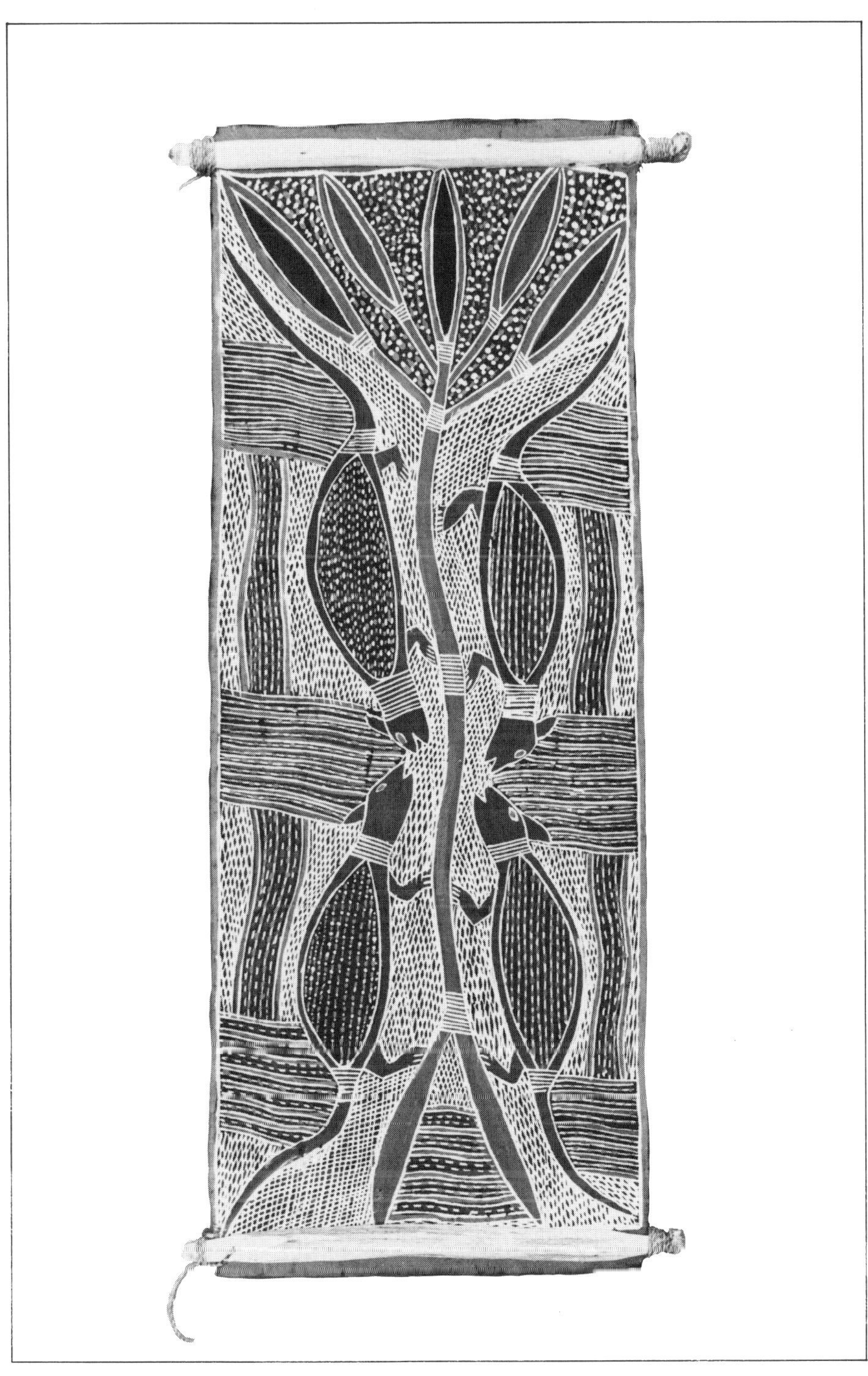

17. **The Wild Plum Tree at Djarrakpi**

Narritjin Maymuru
Yirritja Moiety, Manggalili Clan
Djarrakpi, N.E. Arnhem Land
Ochre on bark
59 x 23 cm
Collection: Mr. James Davidson

Marrngu and his friends feed at the wild plum tree at *Djarrakpi*. The dots among the leaves at the top represent the stones of the wild plum. Horizontal tide marks and vertical bars of parallel dots and dashes indicate Opossum tracks.

18. **Ngapililingu, Ancestral Spirit Woman of the Manggalili**

Narritjin Maymuru
Yirritja Moiety, Manggalili Clan
Djarrakpi, N.E. Arnhem Land
Ochre on bark
79 x 47 cm
Collection: Mr. James Davidson

The figure in this painting is *Ngapililingu,* Ancestral Spirit Woman of the *Manggalili.* On her head is the giant size water carrier made of bark in which she and her band of women helpers, the *Warruthalaku* travelled from Groote Eylandt to the mainland. Above the water carrier is a *Manggalili* symbol for running water. On the water carrier itself six bars of cross hatching form the *Yirritja* triangles. In the centre of this important clan design is a small symbol representing a sacred waterhole. The crossed lines are repeated twice on the body of *Ngapililingu.* On her head she carries a piece of paperbark which she uses to make watercontainers.

In each hand is a 'dragging stick' (*wapitja*) used for stripping the bark from the tree trunk. These important *Manggalili* artefacts are *mariian* (sacred) and were used by the Spirit Woman to make the waterholes for the *Manggalili* people. Besides the 'dragging sticks' are the edible 'yoko' bulbs (black). Six black and eight brown lens shaped symbols are the camping places *Ngapililingu* used while travelling through the country carrying out her work for the *Guwark.* The hatched background represents Opossum tracks, tide marks, and sand dunes.

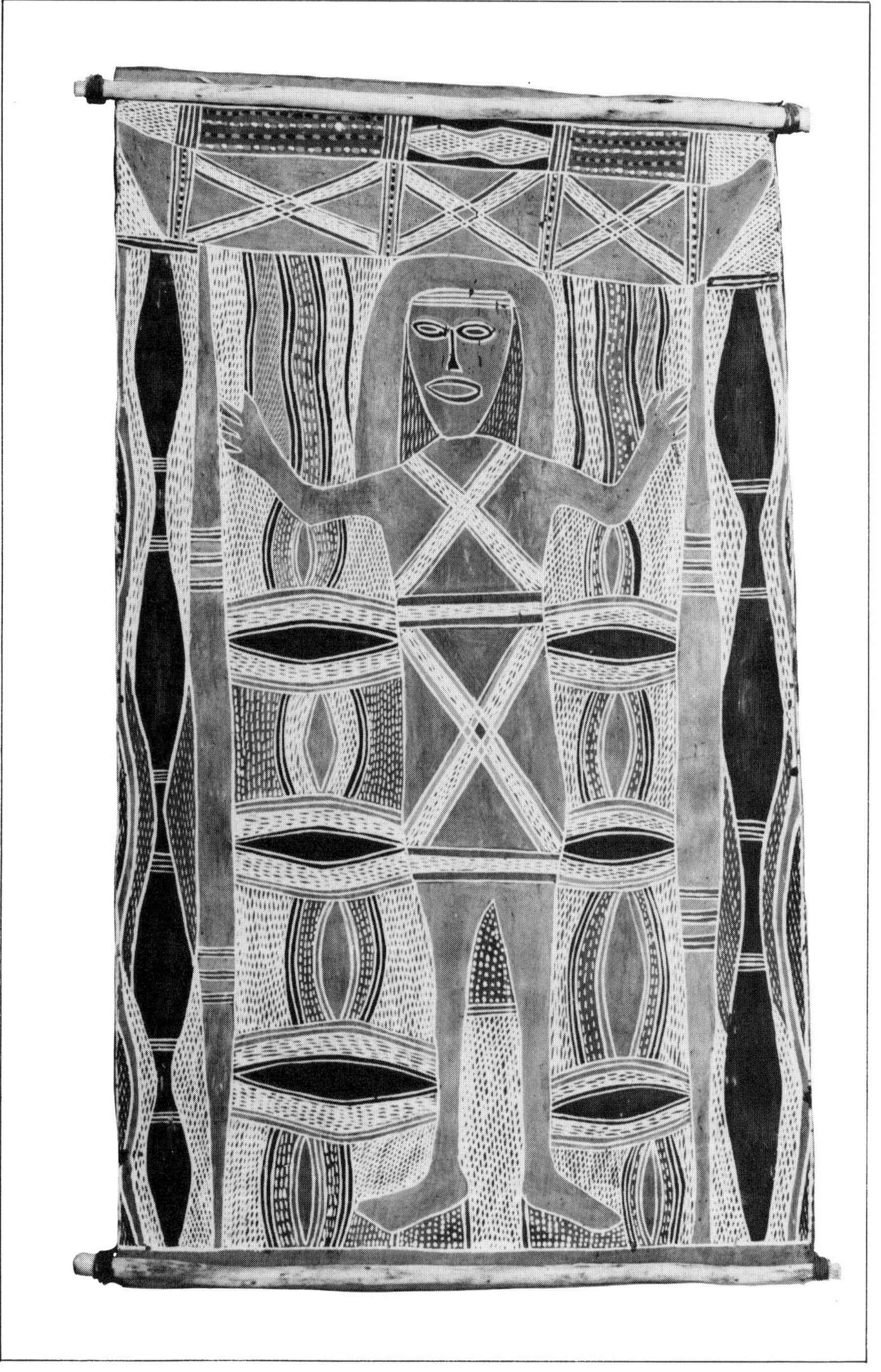

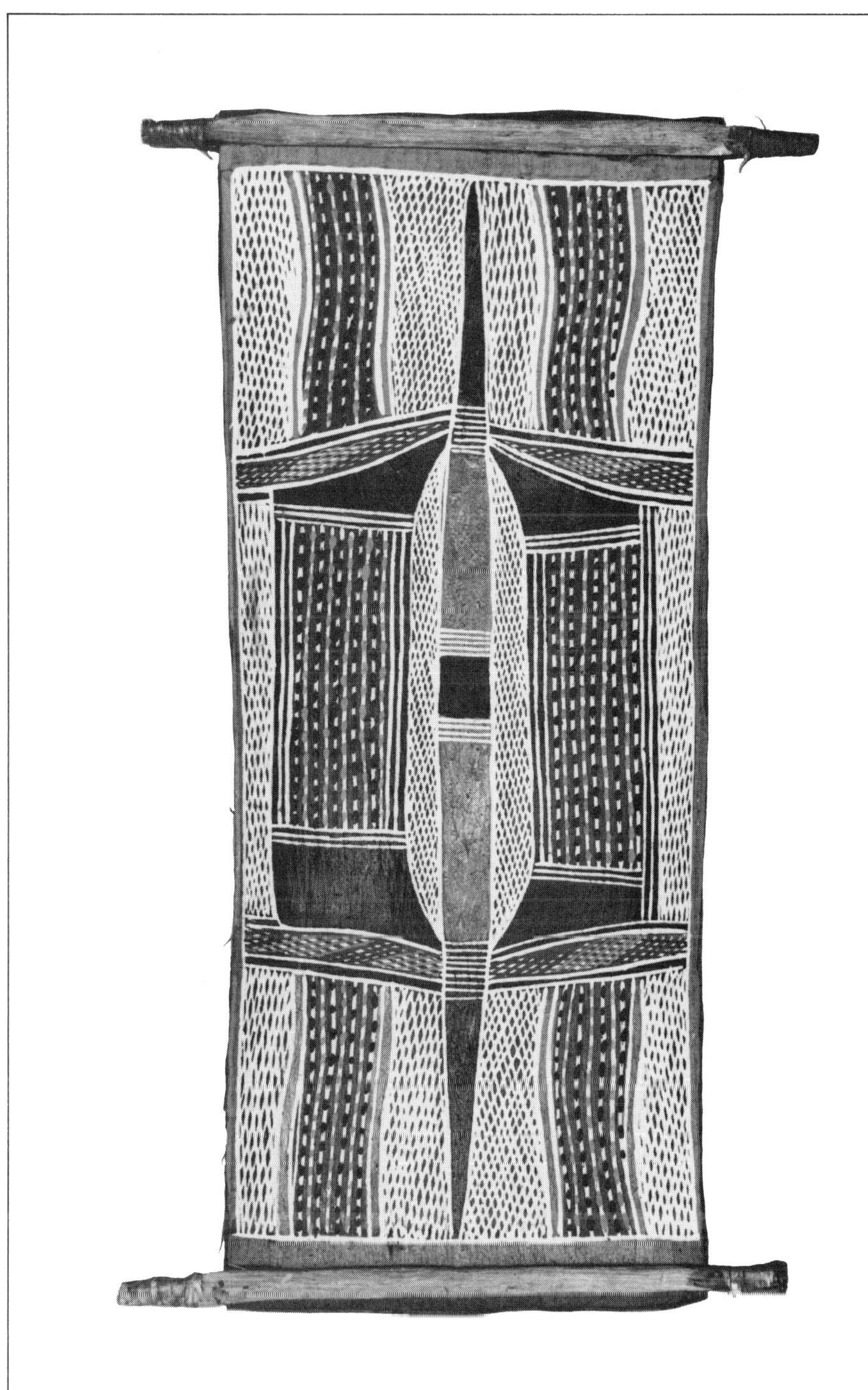

19. Wapitja, Sacred Dragging Stick

Narritjin Maymuru
Yirritja Moiety, Manggalili Clan
Djarrakpi, N.E. Arnhem Land
Ochre on bark
45 x 18 cm
Collection: Mr. James Davidson

Shows the 'sacred dragging stick' (*wapitja*) with a paper bark water container on each side. Opossum tracks are shown, and the cross hatching represents sand dunes. Horizontal bars of cross hatching are the reefs that are the home of *Nguykal,* the Kingfish.

20. Macassan Pipe

Narritjin Maymuru
Yirritja Moiety, Manggalili Clan
Djarrakpi, N.E. Arnhem Land
Wood, decorated with ochre depicting *Marrngu* on both sides, with Opossum tracks and sand hills
45 x 7 x 4 cm (diam.)
Collection: Mr. James Davidson

21. Pair of Woomeras

Narritjin Maymuru
Yirritja Moiety, Manggalili Clan
Djarrakpi, N.E. Arnhem Land
Wood, painted with ochre. Hook shaped to form head of the *Guwark*
77 x 5 x 3.5 cm (diam.)
Collection: Mr. James Davidson

22. Pair of Wapitja, or Sacred Dragging Sticks as used by Ngapililingu

Narritjin Maymuru
Yirritja Moiety, Manggalili Clan
Djarrakpi, N.E. Arnhem Land
Wood, painted with ochre
133 x 2.5 cm (diam.)
Collection: Mr. James Davidson

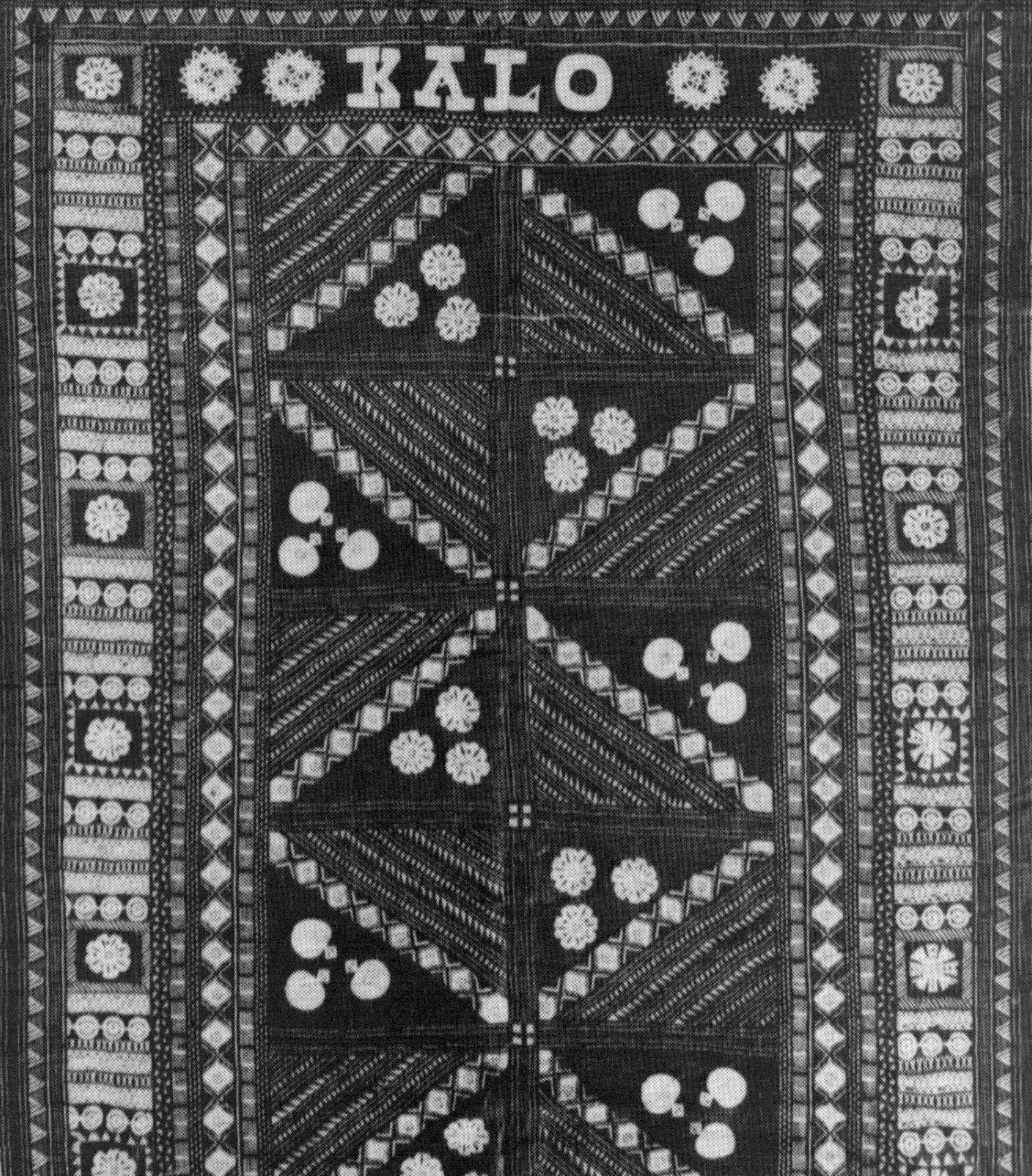

KALO

The Solomon Islands

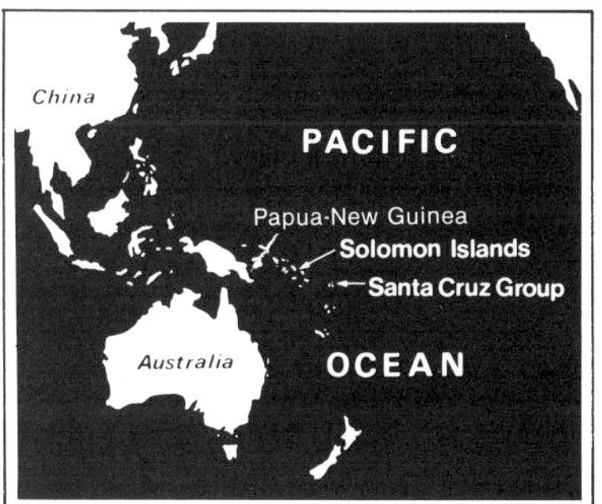

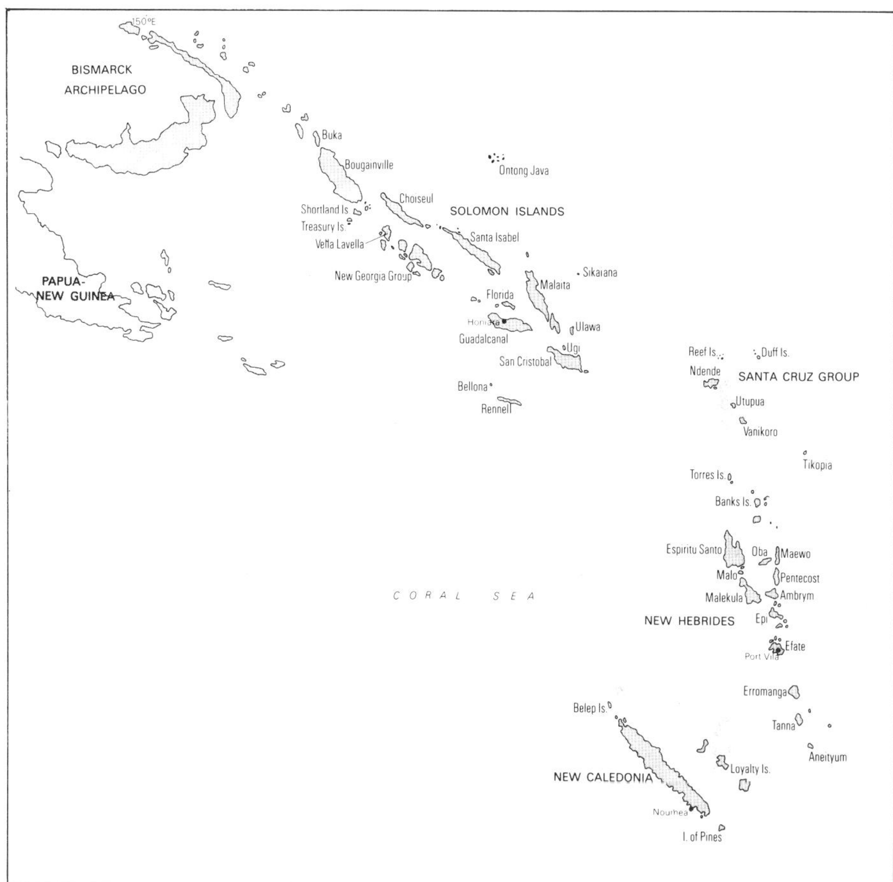

The discriminating application of decoration to small portions of the naked human body echoes the elegant tonal contrasts and fine balancing of plain and patterned surfaces central to the art of the Solomons. Clothing was extremely scanty, usually being restricted to waist and perineal bands for men and rudimentary aprons or skirts for women. But an extensive variety of beautiful ornaments were worn, mainly by men, who artistically adorned their naked or near naked bodies with concentrated patches of pattern and colour. Sweet smelling floral emblems, clusters of tiny beads or swirls of plaited grass bands were delicate natural embellishments to the human body.

Wood or bamboo combs were worn in the hair, the handles carved or incised, or decorated with pearl shell inlay or intricate plaiting of yellow, red and black plant stems, according to region. Ear ornaments inserted into the pierced ear lobe included broad discs, sticks bound with coloured grasswork, wooden plugs, often carved or inlaid, which were gradually increased in size to extend the lobe, and pendants of nut and teeth. Wooden, shell or bone

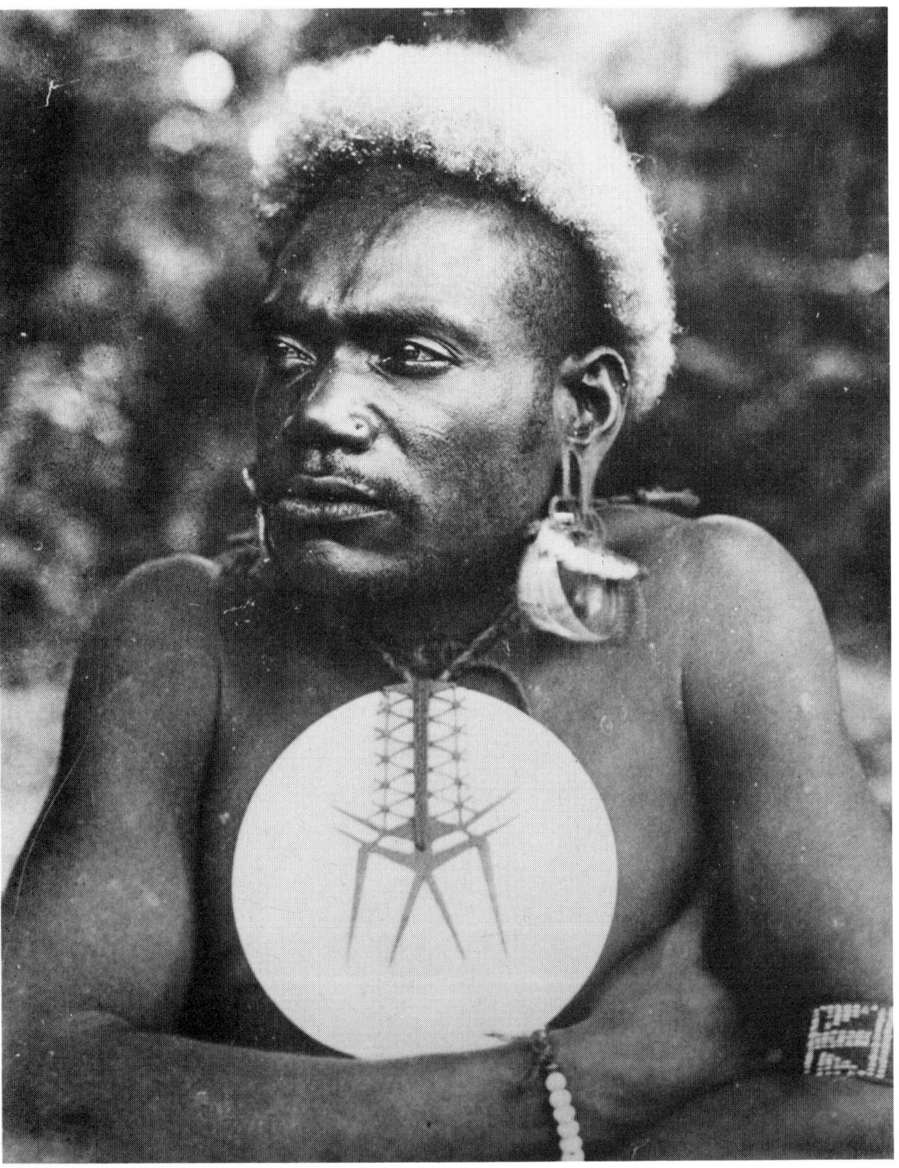

Solomon Islander wearing Breast Ornament by courtesy of the National Museum, Sydney.

pins and discs were worn in the pierced septum of the nose. Flowers and scented plants were used to adorn the hair or tucked into armlets which, like wristlets, were plaited of coloured plant stems. Belts were made of dyed or natural vegetable fibres or composed of white, red and black beads threaded in patterns on to fibre bands. Necklaces were made of seeds, shell beads and teeth of dog, porpoise, cuscus and fruit bat.

The most valued ornaments were fashioned from shell. White cowries strung together were draped across the forehead or around the legs, below the knee. Ornaments known as *Kap Kap* were worn on the forehead or breast; they are discs of turtle shell intricately carved in open work; in Santa Cruz the turle shell overlay is not circular but consists of stylized representations of frigate bird, shark and bonito. The shell discs might also be engraved with blackened designs. Another type of breast pendant is of pearl shell cut into crescent or stylized frigate bird forms.

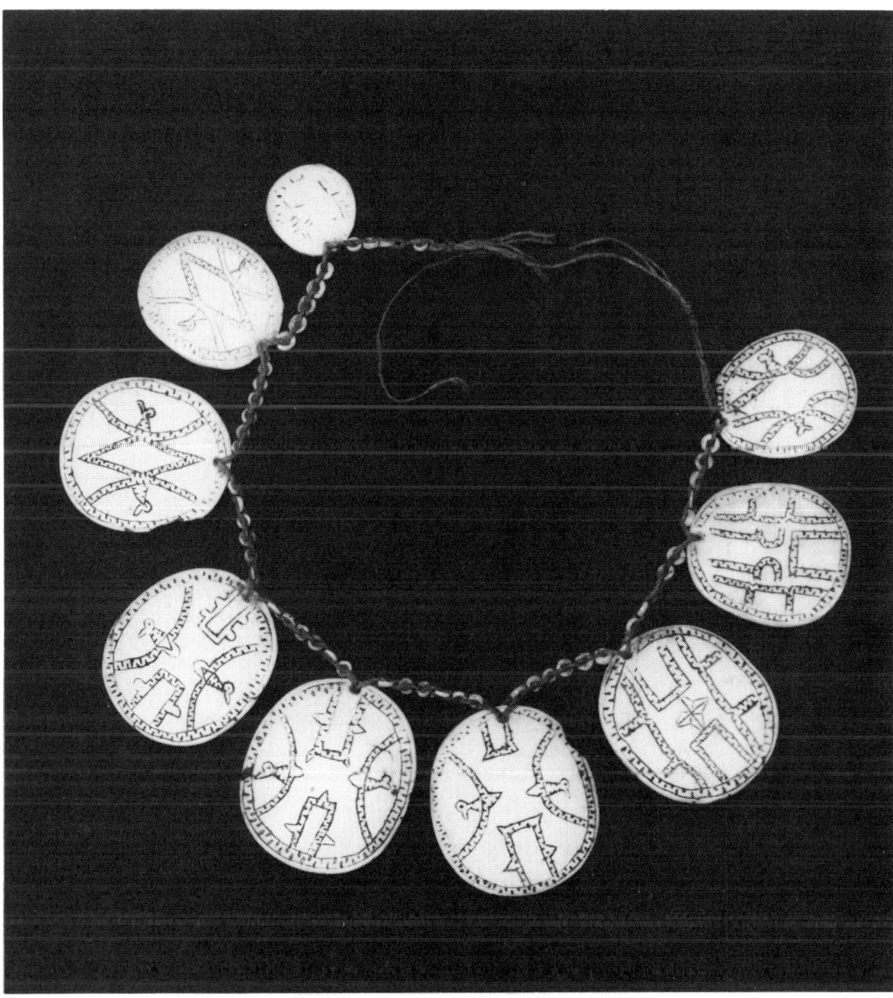

23. Kap Kap Necklace

Solomon Islands
Engraved tridacna shell strung on a
fine twisted natural fibre cord
decorated with cowrie shells
L. 39.4 cm
c. 1900
Collection: National Gallery of Victoria

Pearl and tridacna shell ornaments were used in the Solomon Islands as a medium of exchange in important transactions such as marriage. The bride price was calculated on exact quantities of certain types of jewellery. Shell ornaments such as these with blackened incised designs were worn by the men either on the forehead or the breast. The pattern of the ornament is characteristic of Solomon Islands art motifs where one often finds an extremely graceful, almost naturalistic treatment of bird and fish forms combined with elegant abstract linear patterns. The tonal contrast between the white shell and the dark drawing is the mirror image of the convention used for wood carving, where larger wooden objects such as bowls were coated with a black substance inlaid with delicate designs of white shell

These beautifully worked shell objects were manufactured using simple tools; pump drill, bow saw and stone for breaking and polishing. Armlets, for example, were cut from solid tridacna shell by a laborious process. The thick shell near the hinge was ground to a disc, a hole pecked through the centre and the central portion sawn out with a rattan 'blade', held tight between the two arms of a weighted wood bow.

Judith Ryan
Circulations Officer
National Gallery of Victoria.

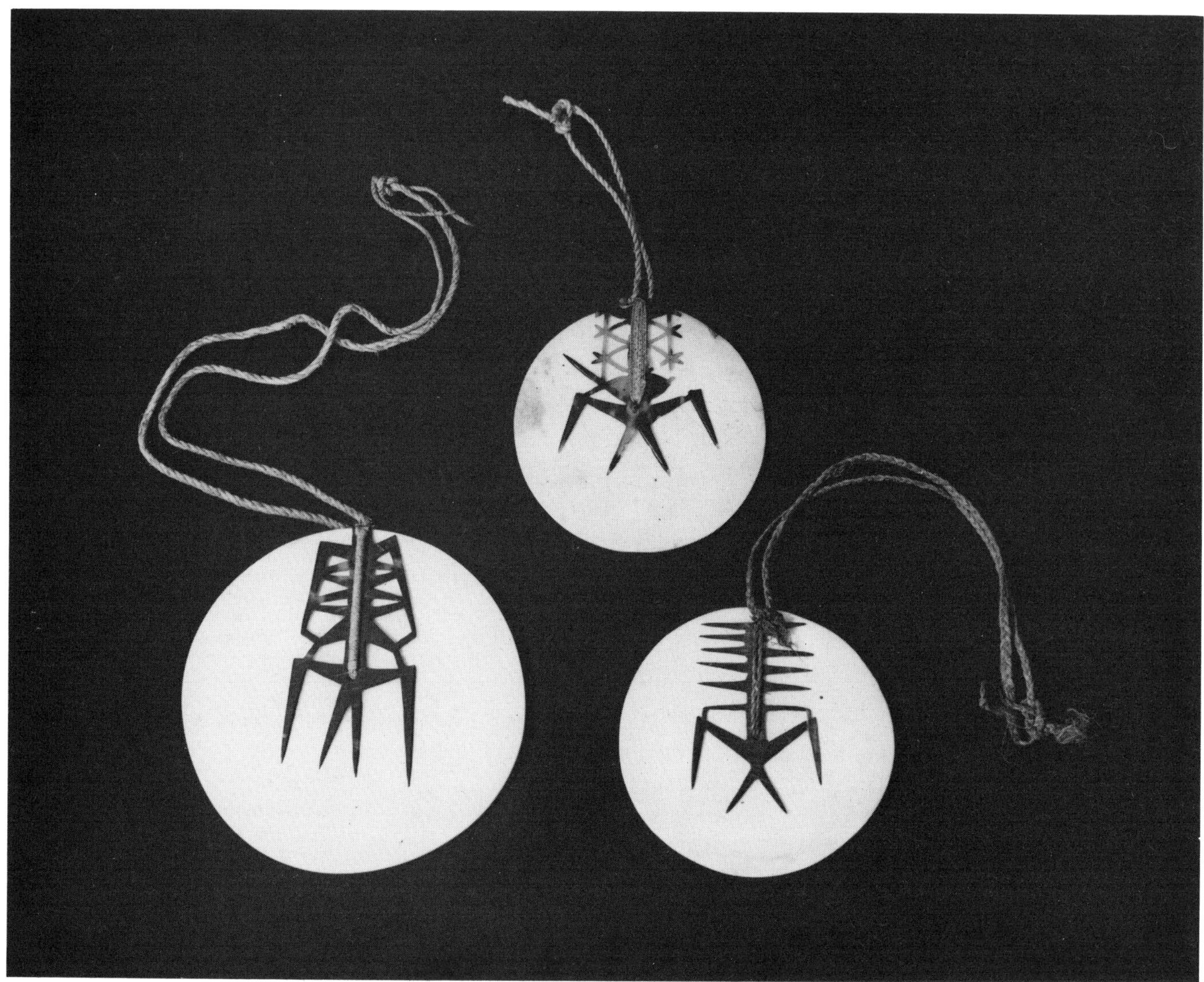

<table>
<tr><td>

24. **Breast Ornament**

Banks Island
Large disc of tridacna shell, overlaid
with a turtle shell plate
11 cm (diam.)
Early 20th century
By courtesy of the National Museum
of Victoria Council

</td><td>

25. **Breast Ornament**

Santa Cruz
Large disc of tridacna shell with turtle
shell overlay
13.7 cm (diam.)
Early 20th century
By courtesy of the National Museum
of Victoria Council

</td><td>

26. **Breast Ornament**

Santa Cruz
Large disc of tridacna shell, overlaid
with turtle shell plate to form simple
silhouetted design
10.4 cm (diam.)
Early 20th century
By courtesy of the National Museum
of Victoria Council

</td></tr>
</table>

27. **Breast Ornament**

Vella Lavella Island, Solomon Islands
Pearl shell, with pierced geometic
decoration; the finial is a flattened
hook with a frigate bird head holding
a fish on either side
4.5 cm x 8.4 cm
Early 20th century
Collection: National Gallery of Victoria

28. **Breast Ornament**

Vella Lavella Island, Solomon Islands
Pearl shell with pierced geometric
decoration; with two pairs of frigate
bird heads and a double loop of red
and blue beads
6.5 cm x 9.5 cm
Early 20th century
Collection: National Gallery of Victoria

29. **Breast Ornament**

Vella Lavella Island, Solomon Islands
Pearl shell with pierced geometric
decoration and distinctive concentric
ring formation
6.3 cm x 5.9 cm
Early 20th century
Collection: National Gallery of Victoria

30. **Breast Ornament**

Vella Lavella Island, Solomon Islands
Pearl shell rather roughly fashioned
with pierced geometic decoration
5.4 cm x 7.5 cm
Early 20th century
Collection: National Gallery of Victoria

31. **Breast Ornament**

Vella Lavella Island, Solomon Islands
Pearl shell with pierced geometric
decoration
6.4 cm x 7.2 cm
Early 20th century
Collection: National Gallery of Victoria

32. **Ear Plug**

Solomon Islands
Bamboo decorated with linear
geometric designs
16 cm x 1 cm (diam.)
c. 1890
Collection: Mr. James Davidson

33. **Nose Ring**

Solomon Islands
Tridacna shell
5.5 cm (diam.)
c. 1890
Collection: Mr. James Davidson

34. **Nose Plug**

Solomon Islands
Tridacna shell
11.5 cm x 1.5 cm (diam.)
c. 1890
Collection: Mr. James Davidson

35. **Pair of Fish Hooks**

Choiseul, Solomon Islands
Wooden shank lined with pearl shell,
turtle shell barb, natural fibre
attachments
7.7 cm x 1.2 cm
Early 20th century
Collection: National Gallery of Victoria

36. **Bowl**

Southern Solomon Islands
Wood inlaid with pearl shell. The
polished black hemisphere is
delicately decorated with pearl
triangles, crosses and teardrops.
Such wooden bowls were standard
household utensils, generally used for
serving food
25 cm (diam.)
20th century
Collection: National Gallery of Victoria

37. **Lime Container**

Choiseul, Solomon Islands
Bamboo decorated with linear
geometric designs, inlaid with pearl
shell
18.5 cm x 4 cm (diam.)
Early 20th century
Collection: National Gallery of Victoria

Betel chewing, widely known in
Melanesia, is practised throughout the
Solomon Islands. The mixture consists
of a nut of the areca palm, a fruit or
leaves of the betel pepper, and lime
made from burned coral or shell. It
has a stimulating effect and
minimises hunger and fatigue. The
lime is kept in gourds or bamboo
containers, often exquisitely
decorated, and a wooden or bone
stick, moistened by being drawn
between the lips, is used to take it.
Small wooden mortars are used for
crushing areca nuts by old people
who have lost their teeth.

38. **Lime Stick**

Admiralty Islands
Wood carved with pair of figures
50.8 cm x 2.5 cm
20th century
Collection: National Gallery of Victoria

39. **Spear Point**

Admiralty Islands
Painted wood with overmodelled and
painted fibre and sting ray spine
57.1 cm x 2.7 cm (diam.)
Early 20th century
Private Collection, Melbourne

40. **Kap Kap**

New Ireland
Disc of tridacna shell, overlaid with
filigree disc of turtle shell. Such
prestigious ornaments, as in Santa
Cruz were worn on the chest
10.5 cm (diam.) x 0.3 cm d.
19th century
Private Collection, Melbourne

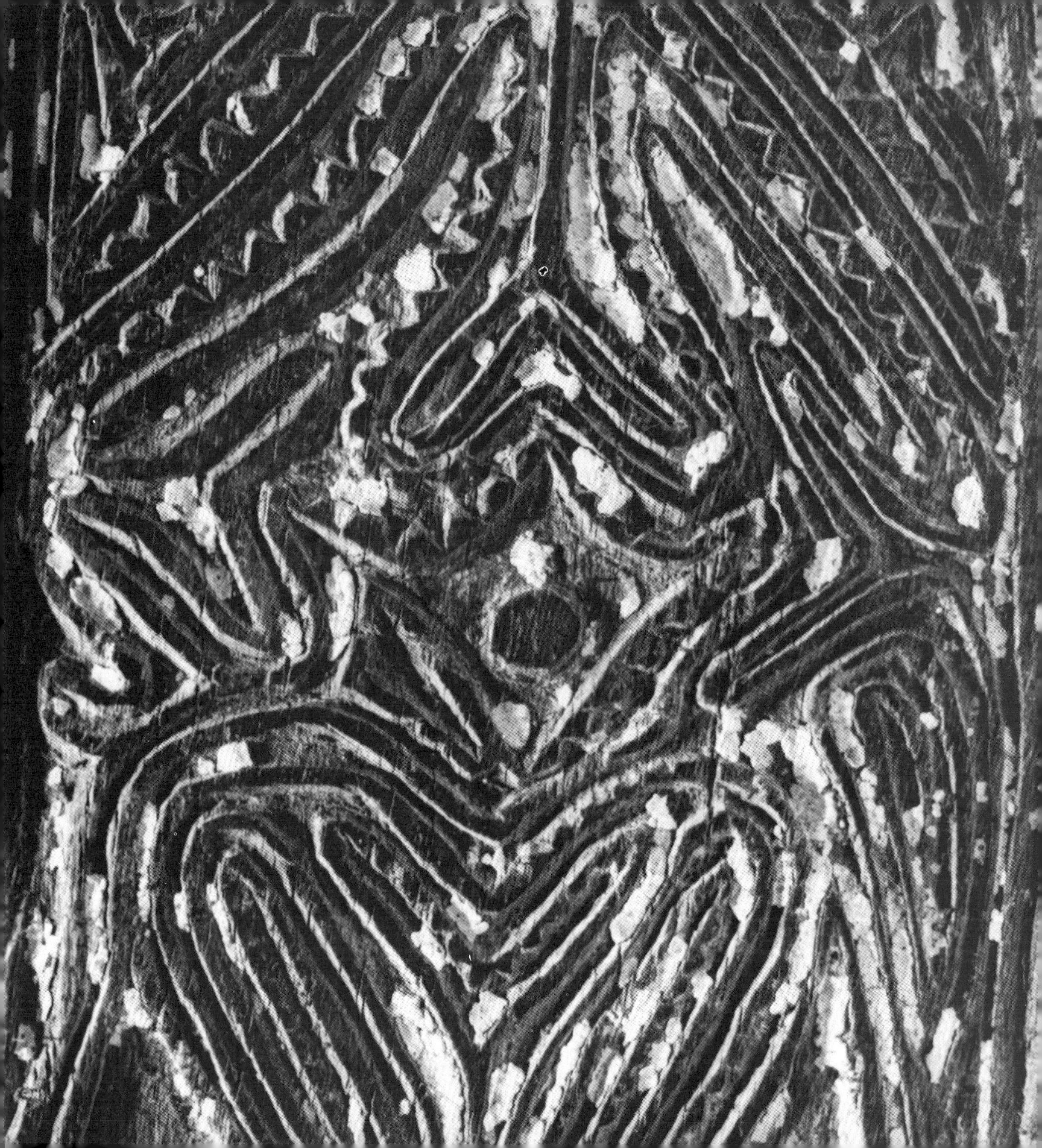

New Guinea

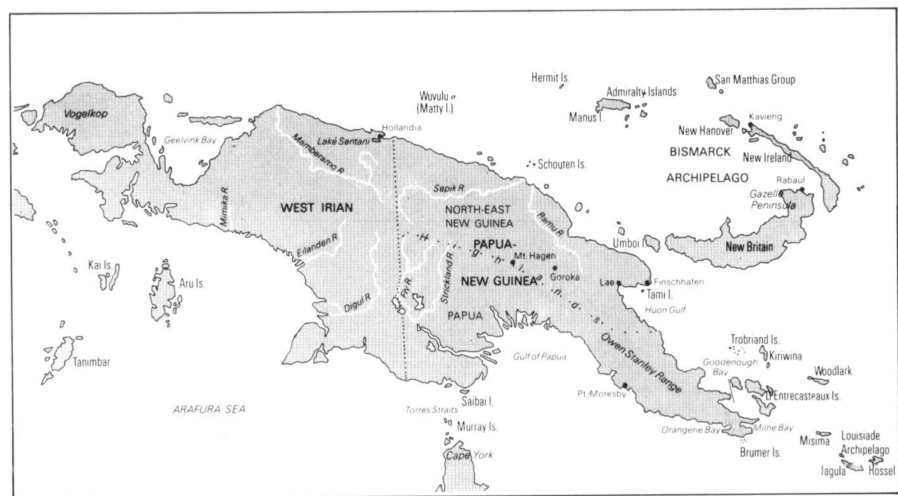

New Guinea, the largest island of Oceania, has produced the greatest number and variety of art objects of the entire Pacific basin. The art of New Guinea's eleven major culture areas can be divided into two basic categories. In the first, sculptural form is often overpowered by intricate, decorative surface ornamentation. Colour is sparingly applied and the two dimensional, linear designs, though characteristically curvilinear, are symmetrical and carefully controlled. This urbane, sophisticated geometry of pattern and tonal contrast echoing the art of the Solomons is best illustrated by works from the Massim area, the Huon Gulf and most styles of the western part of the island. The animated yet refined outlining of scrolls, meanders and arabesques constitutes a style of linear energy, grace and elegance.

The second, strangely potent expression rises like a firebrand in the art of the Sepik River, intense in its exaggerated emphasis on three dimensional forms which are conceived in full rhythms. In this complex dramatic sculpture, surface ornament, whether carved or painted, serves to accentuate sculptural mass. It is as if the sculptor is attempting to embody three dimensionally the dynamic elements of his environment; thus animal, bird and man interpenetrate in weird conjunctions. Bird's beak, nose and penis meet in a forceful, angular, elongated thrust of spiritual tension, or man is surmounted by a protective bird or subsumed into the shape of a crocodile.

As in Aboriginal art, there is a dynamic interrelationship between the artist, his natural environment and the mythology of the tribe. Art is born of this harmony accentuated by the use of natural materials, whether bark, ochres, twig brushes or wood, pigments and stone tools, or grasses, fibres, feathers and shell. It is moving to trace the repetition of traditional forms, motifs, colours and decorative patterns unique to each region which stand as fixed constants or points of stasis in a world of blinding and shuddering cultural changes. It is to be hoped that these emblems of nature are not annihilated by greedy, crushing materialism.

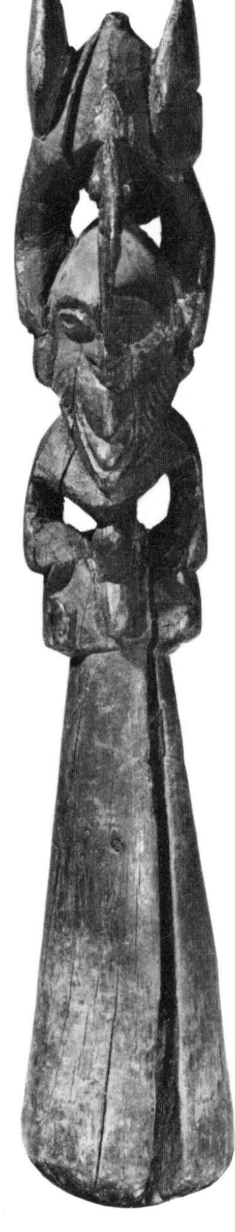

41

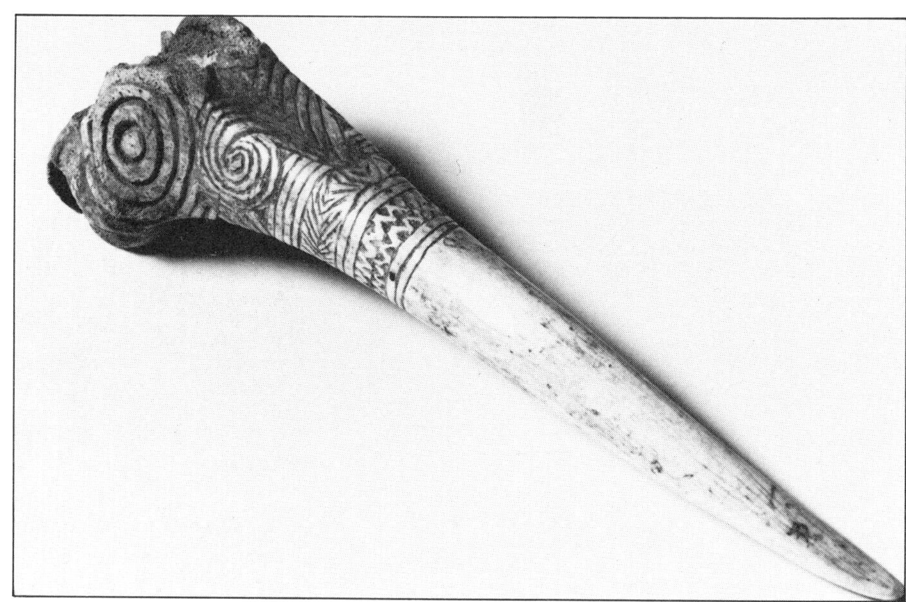

42

Just as bark painting from North East Arnhem Land represents no more than the tip of the mighty iceberg which constitutes Aboriginal art, likewise the carved wooden objects from the Sepik convey only the tiniest fraction of the area's output. For Sepik artists were skilful in other media. The art of basketry was well developed, dance masks and monumental house masks being intricately woven to form sculptures of nightmarish power. Clay was inventively modelled to make cooking pots pulsating with human and animal forms. Roof ornaments in the form of human heads or figures and free standing figures were also made of clay.

The environment of swamp and jungle supplied a great variety of materials that were combined to decorate completed carvings. Bird feathers, vegetable matter such as leaves, seeds, reed, bark and fibres, cowry and nassa shell, snail opercula, human hair, animal fur, reptile skin, bone, teeth and tusks as well as human and animal skulls were drawn together in intriguing collages or used to decorate the human body. Unfortunately most of the carvings visible today in museum context have lost their colourful ceremonial adornments and resemble 'noble ruins', or monuments undressed during the course of time. Pigments were widely available. Black and grey were obtained from mixing charcoal with water and nut oil, white was formed of quicklime from shell, and yellow and reds were derived from natural earths. Vegetable dyes were used to decorate bark cloths and mats.

Wood carving was done exclusively by men. All of the preparatory work was done with an adze possessing a blade of hard, fine grained, volcanic stone or heavy tridacna shell. Details and incisions were then carved with various smaller tools armed with points of teeth from marsupials, rats and sharks. Boars' tusks and awls of bird bone were used for the same purpose. After carving, the wood was often smoothed with sand or shark skin, and sometimes polished with stone or further rubbed by hand with nut oil. Although metal tools speed up this laborious process considerably, they produce much harsher details and tend to isolate the carver from the process of creation.

Judith Ryan
Circulations Officer
National Gallery of Victoria.

41. Pounder, probably used for Sago

Schouten Island, Papua New Guinea
Wood
44 cm x 8 cm
Early 20th century
Collection: National Gallery of Victoria

The pounder or pestle is an essential
household tool in the simple village
societies of the Sepik area and its off-
lying islands; Schouten Island being a
small island to the west of the Sepik
delta. The style seems influenced by
the figure carving of the lower Sepik.
The face is schematized and more
sparsely carved than in Sepik figures.
The body has shrunk to a trunk-like
organic form and the exaggerated
limbs give the figure a powerful aura.
The horn bill bird is beautifully carved,
a recognition by the carver of its
super-human strength. Such birds
play an important role in the magico-
religious traditions of these people
and also in the art of the nearby
Aitape District. In fact bird, animal
and human motifs are often strangely
yoked together in New Guinea art.

42. Coconut Scraper

Middle Sepik River
Cassoway bone
21 cm long
20th century
Collection: National Gallery of Victoria

The Sepik inhabitants' intense love for
art is reflected in their decoration of
virtually every implement in common
use. Lime calabashes, bamboo
spatulas, bone daggers, coconut
scrapers and spoons, food
suspension hooks — all are covered
with purely ornamental or
anthropomorphic patterns having the
most graceful curved treatment.

43. Arm Guard

Aibom, Middle Sepik River
Tortoiseshell with graceful incised
decoration
15.0 cm h. x 25.0 cm (diam.)
20th century
Collection: National Gallery of Victoria

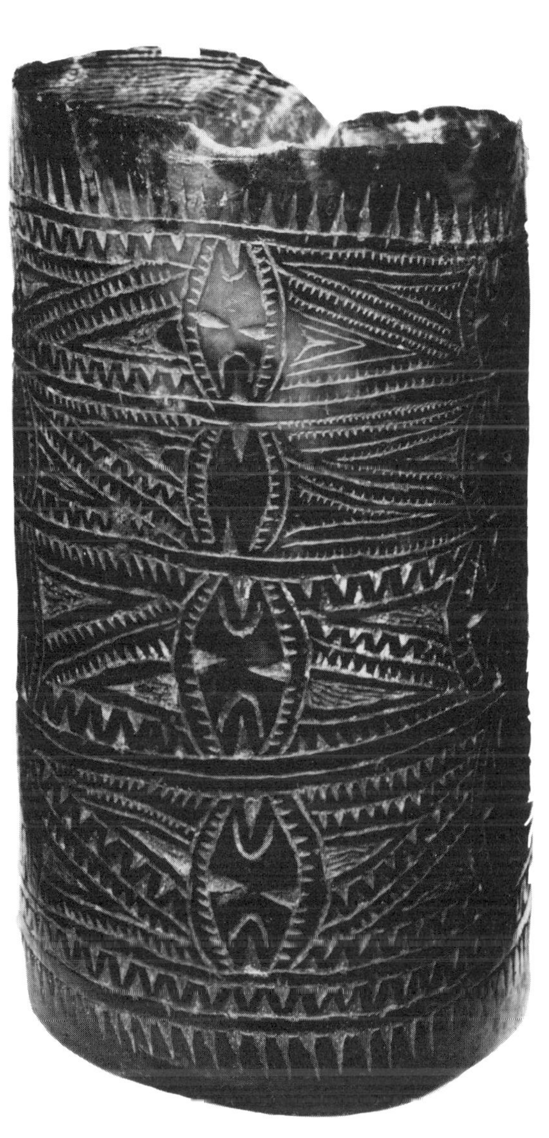

43

44. **Male Ancestor Figure**

Lower Ramu River
Wood
22.0 cm h.
20th century
Collection: National Gallery of Victoria

The human form is the dominant motif
in Sepik art and is most commonly
conceived with an enlarged head,
elongated torso and relatively
shortened limbs. Also characteristic is
the exaggeration of the nose, which in
some instances is flattened and
bulbous, and in others is elongated in
imitation of a bird beak. Certain types
even terminate in bird heads to
intensify the relationship to the animal
prototype. In such simplified plastic
images of the human form, surface
ornament is minimized, and colour,
mostly red or white, is usually only
applied monochromatically rather
than in patterns.

45. **Tambaran Figure**

Middle Sepik River
Wood with traces of pigment
26.0 cm h. x 4.0 cm w.
Early 20th century
Collection: National Gallery of Victoria

46. **Canoe Prow**

Murik Lagoon
Wood with traces of lime
45.2 cm l.
Early 20th century
Collection: National Gallery of Victoria

47. **Head Rest**

Sepik River
Wood, stone carved with finely
incised long meanders, circles and
chevron patterns on its underside.
The bamboo supports are missing
32.9 cm l.
Late 19th-early 20th century
Collection: National Gallery of Victoria

Decoration of such mundane objects
caused constant awareness of the
presence of the supernatural and its
potential involvement in everyday life
as well as during formal religious
observations.

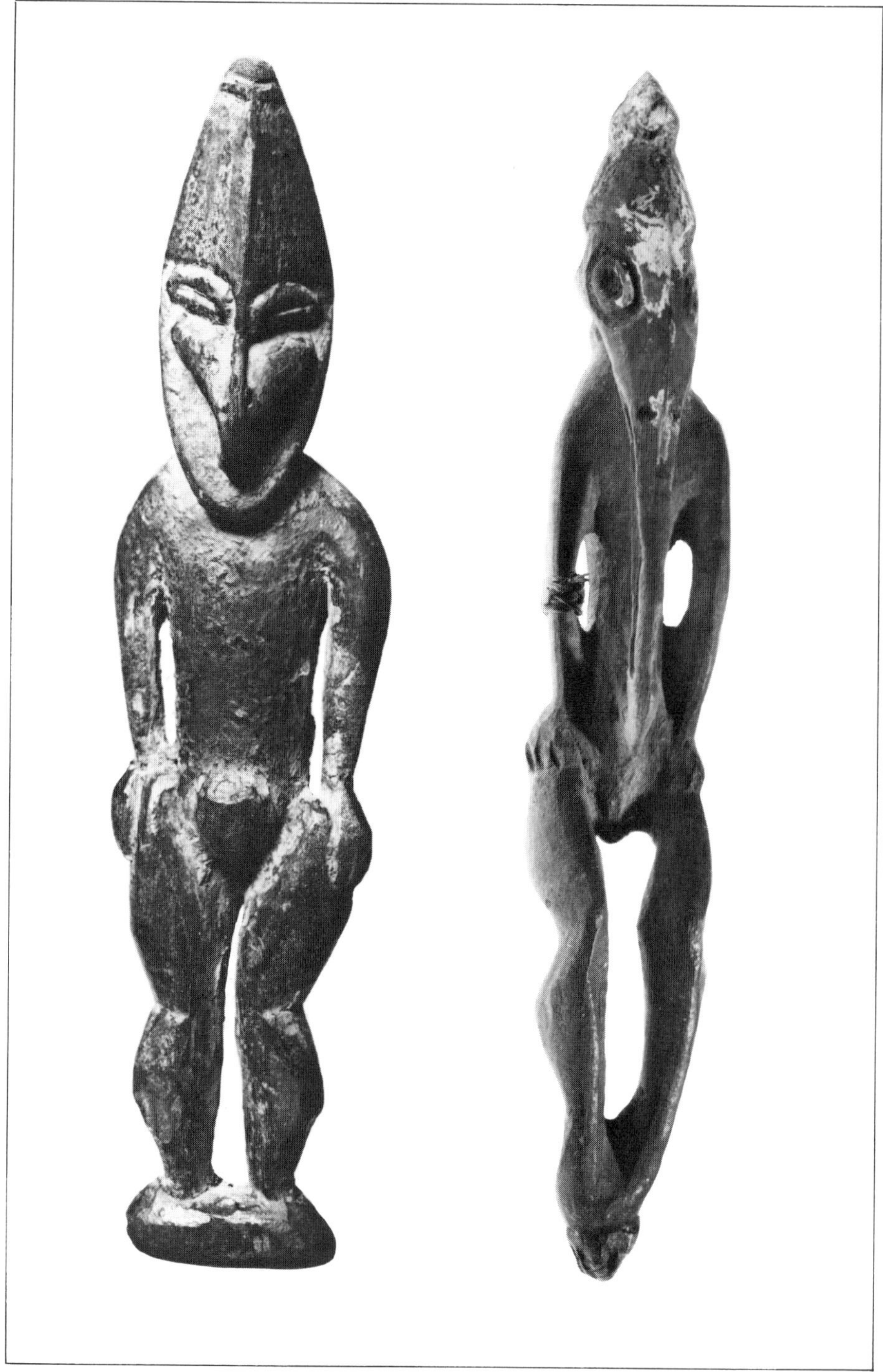

44

45

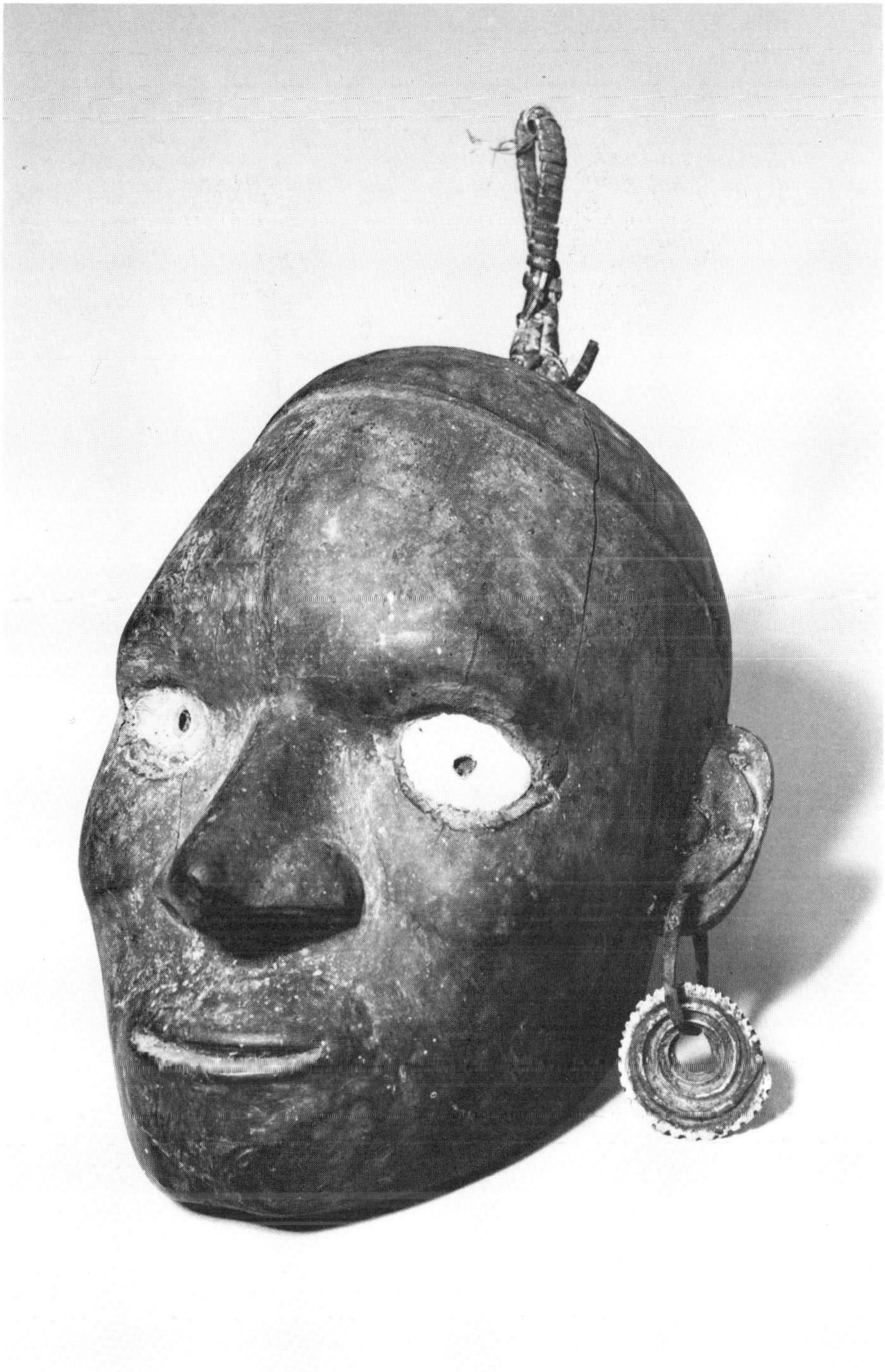

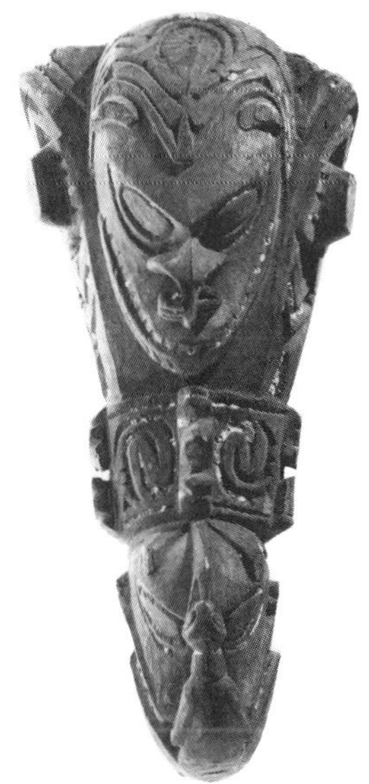

46

48. **Figurative Carving**

Sepik River
Wood
48.3 cm h.
20th century
Collection: National Gallery of Victoria

Such columnar integration of human
and bird motifs is a miniature version
of the towering house posts common
in the architectural carving of the
area.

49. **Carved Head and Necklaces**

Lake Chambri
Wood and shell
28 cm x 17.5 cm
20th century
Collection: National Gallery of Victoria

Of astonishing naturalism and
plasticity, this refined head is a
dignified echo of the overmodelled
human skulls commonly used in
funerary and fertility ceremonies;
possibly serving as a substitute for a
modelled skull which has been lost.
Such skulls, of dead ancestors or
head hunting victims, were modelled
over in clay, and decorated with
shells, human hair and pigments
imitating the facial painting of the
deceased.

49

50. **Net Drying Hook**

Sepik River
Wood incised with simple geometric
patterns
26.8 cm x 15.5 cm
20th century
Collection: National Gallery of Victoria

51. **Lime Tube Stopper**

Middle Sepik River
Cassowary bone, top carved with
crouching bird motif.
30.5 cm x 11.5 cm
Early 20th century
Collection: National Gallery of Victoria

Such carvings were made for
presentation to an initiate by his
mother's brother. Lime, which was
carried in a bamboo container, was
eaten with betel nuts.

52. **Lime Tube Stopper**

Middle Sepik River
Cassowary bone, top carved with
crouching bird motif
28 cm x 9 cm
Early 20th century
Collection: National Gallery of Victoria

53. **Betel Mortar**

Lower Sepik
Wood
16.1 cm h. x 8.5 cm d. (irreg.)
19th century
Private Collection, Melbourne

54. **Betel Mortar**

Lower Ramu River
Wood
13.2 cm h. x 6.8 cm d.
Early 20th century
Private Collection, Melbourne

55. **Group of Lime Spatulae**

Massim area
Wood, incised surface patterns
heightened with lime
20th century
Collection: National Gallery of Victoria

These implements form a necessary
part of the equipment of betel
chewing, a practice which is wide
spread in Melanesia. Betel is the
mildly intoxicating fruit of the betel
palm found widely throughout the
Pacific, which is chewed mixed with
various other substances, including
lime. The special tools used for this
practice are often highly artistic. In
the Sepik, some of the mortars used
to grind various components of the
concoction are embellished with
striking human figure motifs, although
the bone lime spatulae tend to be
simpler and less inventive.

In the Massim area the reverse is
true; the mortars are fairly plain
whereas the spatulae are covered
with voluptuous linear curving
designs. This is possibly because the
mortar is a more suitable vehicle for
three dimensional carving and the
spatula is ideally shaped for the
exploitation of two dimensional
incised surface decoration.
Interestingly, as these spatulae
ranked high in the prestige of
ownership, the grandiosity of the
design of the handle occasionally
rendered them virtually useless as
functional objects.

Massim art is concerned primarily
with surface ornament rather than
with the problems of developing
sculpture in the round, an affinity it
shares with the nearby Admiralty and
Solomon Islands. Figures are stylized,
being subordinate to the elegantly
placed scrolling incised designs,
originally heightened with lime.
Whereas in Sepik River art there is a
constant stress on three dimensional,
plastic forms, concentrated in silent,
haunting shapes or charged with
spiritual tension through distortion.
The human motif is the prime focus of
Sepik art, whether conceived as
towering monument, graphic mask or
wiry hook figure.

Massim hard wood carving is distinct
from Sepik carving in that the full
flowering of the tradition possibly post
dates the introduction of steel tools.
The even, flowing appearance of the
refined linear patterns would be
particularly difficult to achieve with
stone or bone tools.

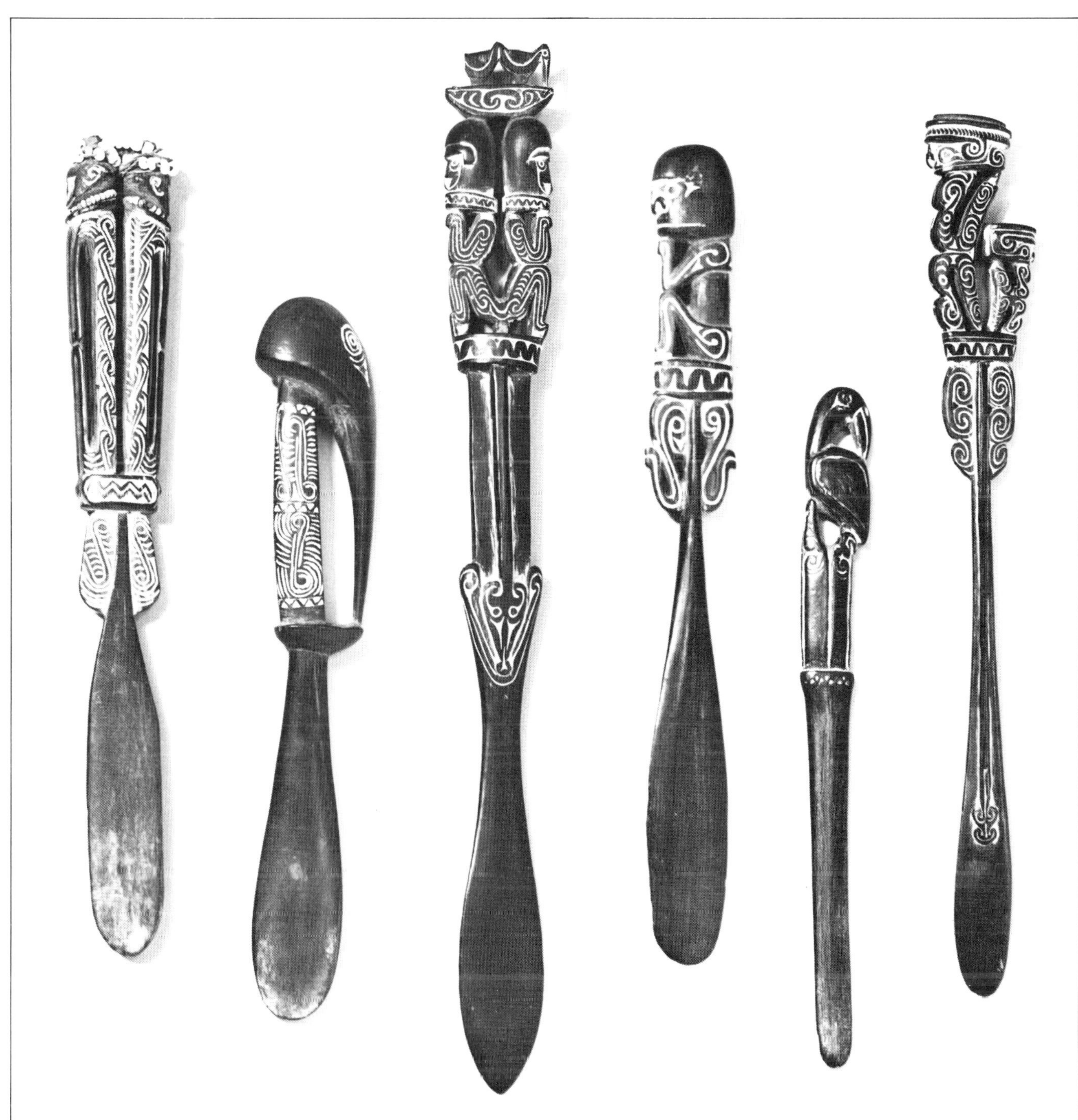

56. **Sago Peg**

Maprik area
Wood with traces of colour
60.0 cm h. x 5.5 cm w. x 4.5 cm d.
20th century
Private Collection, Melbourne

57. **Sago Peg**

Maprik area
Wood with woven wrapping
50.4 cm h. x 3.5 cm w. x 4.5 cm d.
20th century
Private Collection, Melbourne

58. **Ceremonial House Decoration**

Maprik area
Wood painted with natural ochres
72.4 cm h. x 26.3 cm w. x 10.0 cm d.
c. 1974
Private Collection, Melbourne

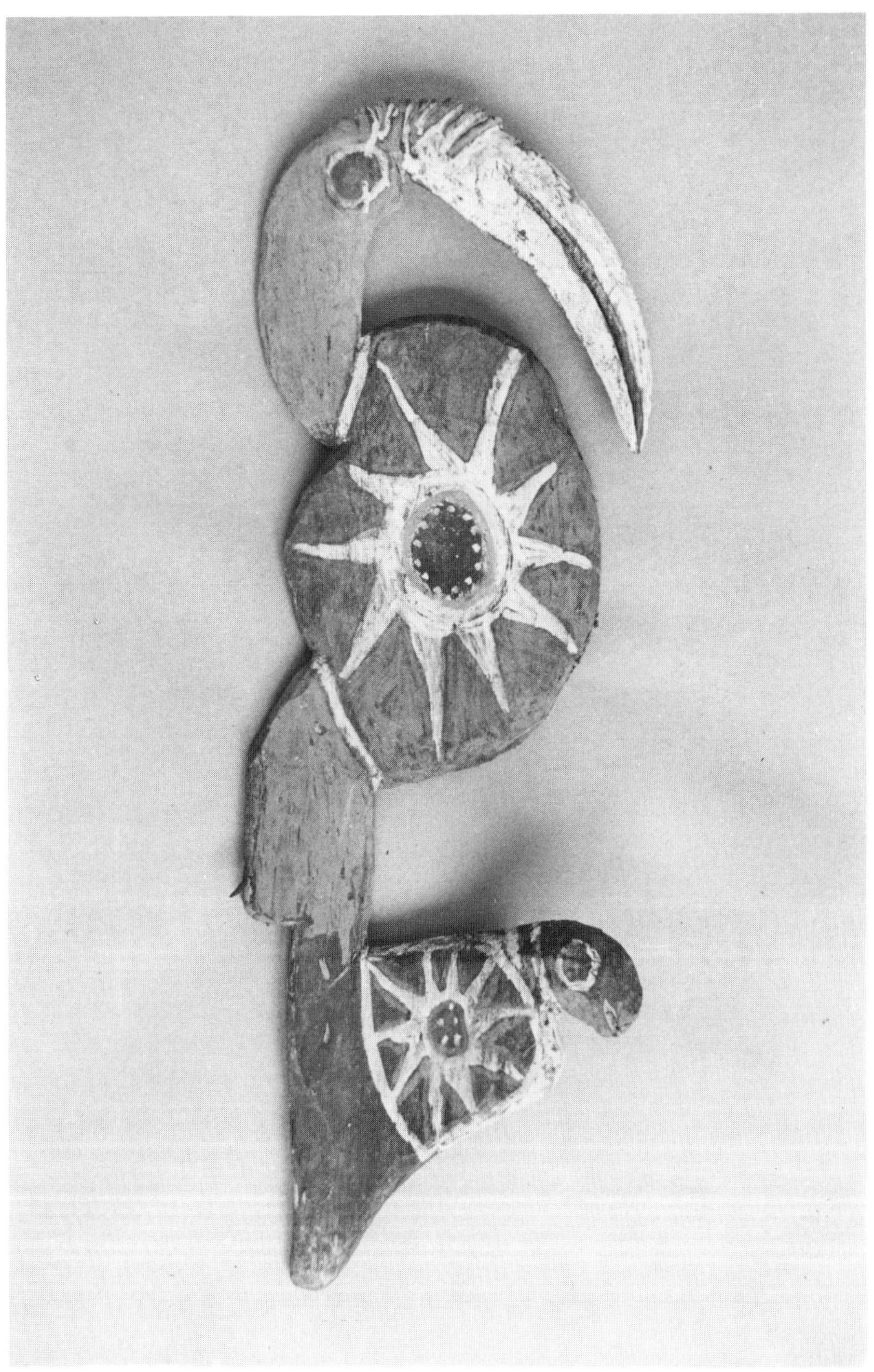

58

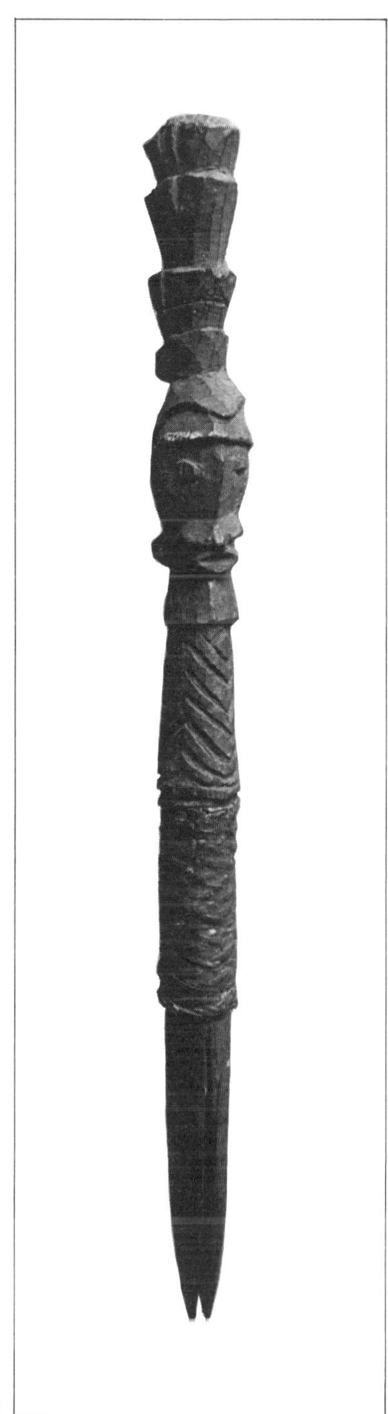

57

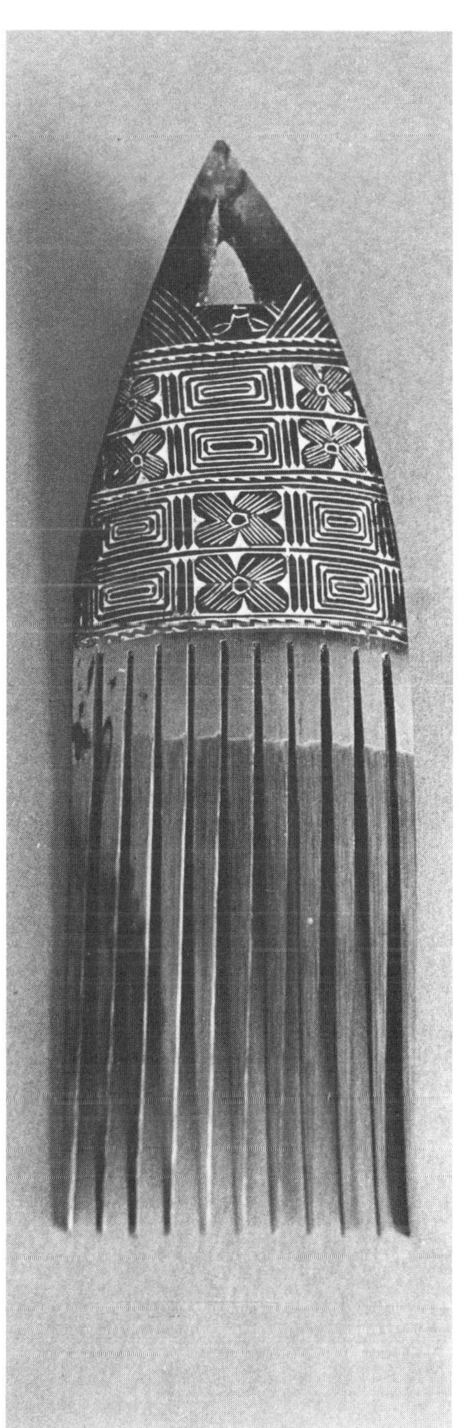

60

59. **Hair Comb**

Kalabu II Village, Abelam
Bamboo, incised with traces of the original lime filling. The design consists of alternating wavy line and coiled meander motif. The top of the comb has a semi-circle with four triangular divisions.
19 cm x 6 cm
Early 20th century
Collection: Michael Hiscock

60. **Comb**

Huon Gulf
Bamboo with incised floral design heightened with lime
27.5 cm h. x 8.0 cm w. x 2.5 cm d.
c. 1970
Private Collection, Melbourne

61. **Betel Mortar**

Huon Gulf
Wood
18.6 cm h. x 5.0 cm (diam.) (irreg.)
20th century
Private Collection, Melbourne

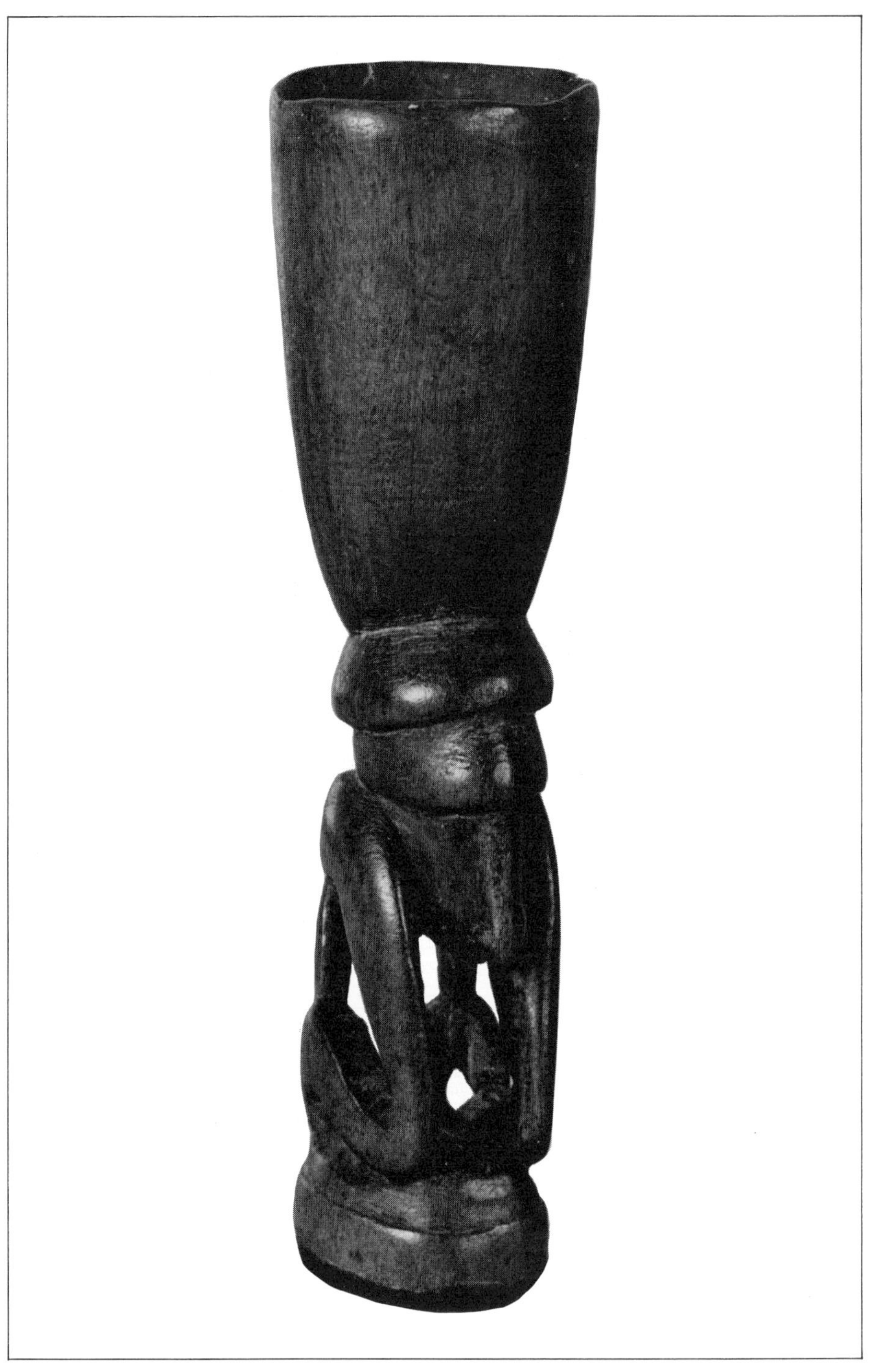

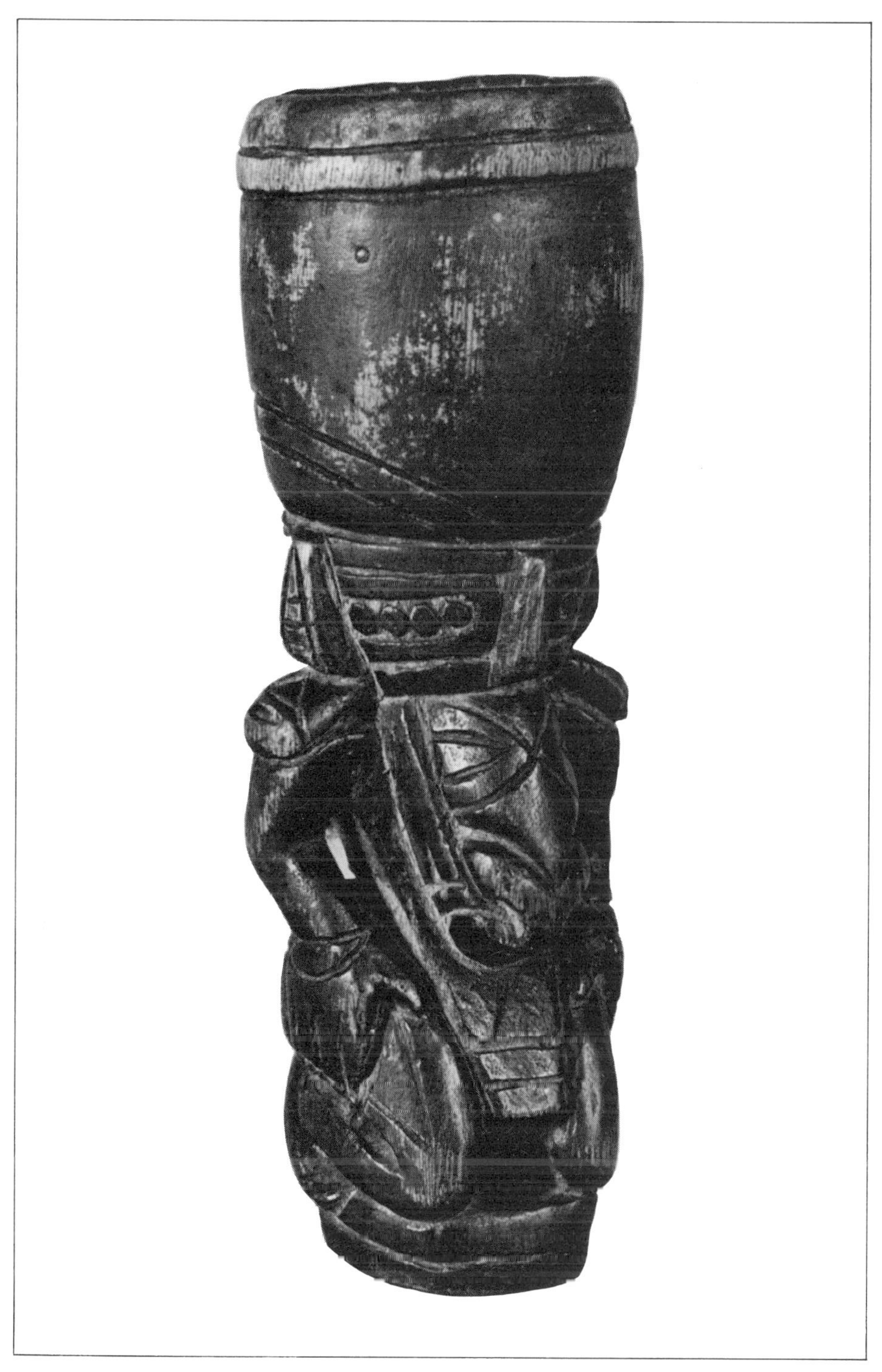

62. **Betel Mortar**

Huon Gulf
Wood
16.2 cm h. x 5.7 cm w. x 5.0 cm d.
20th century
Private Collection, Melbourne

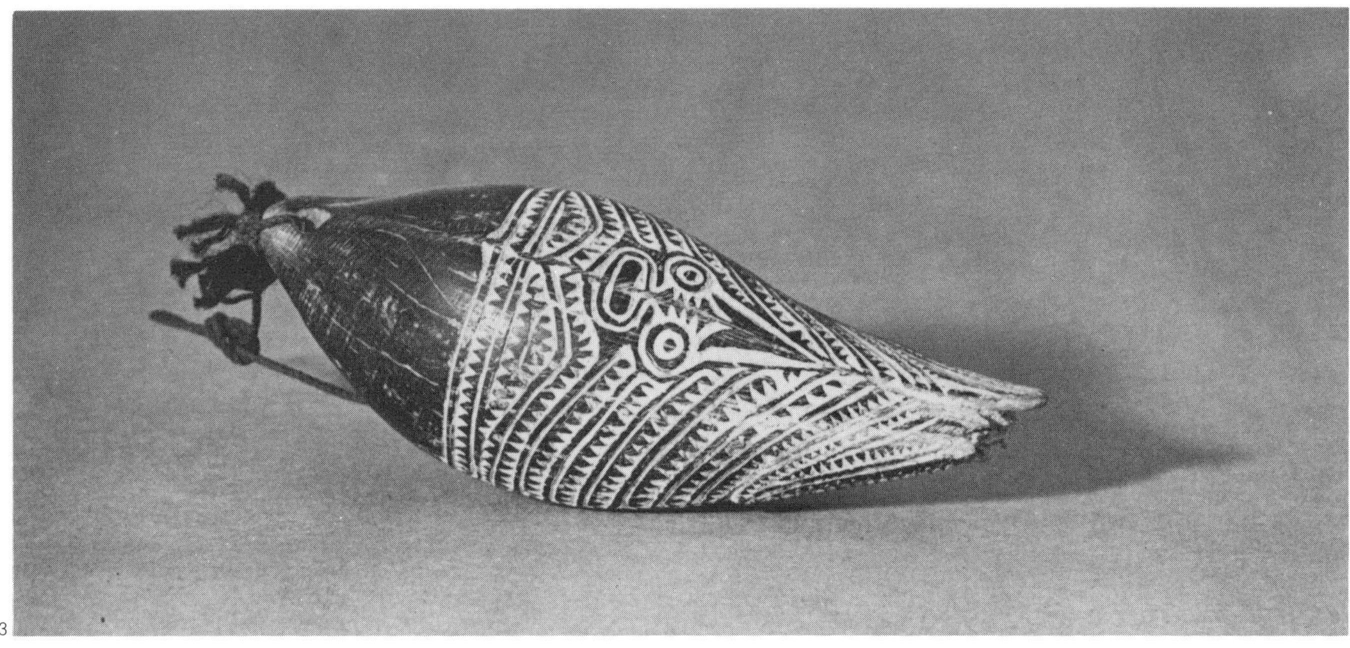

63.

63. Sorcerer's Charm (Marupai)

Papuan Gulf
Carved baby coconut, incised design
heightened with lime
15.4 cm l. x 5.3 cm (diam.)
20th century
Private Collection, Melbourne

64. Head Hunting Horn

Jimi, of Asu Village
Asmat
Bamboo
38 x 5.5 cm (diam.)
20th century
By courtesy of the Macleay Museum

Wood plays a dominant role in the life
of the Asmat echoing their creation
myth that man was actually made out
of wood. There is a clear relationship
between wood, carving and creativity,
a strong identity of man and tree and
each wood carver partakes of some
of the sacredness of *Fumeripits*, the
Great Wood Carver and Great
Headhunter who originated many
Asmat traditions.

Horns are made of segments of
heavy bamboo with one end removed
and the other pierced to make a
mouthpiece. They were blown
especially on headhunting raids to
frighten and paralyse the enemy.
After a successful raid they were
blown triumphantly by the returning
headhunters to inform the villagers of
the results. Horns are usually
decorated with matching reverse zig
zags which meet each other to form
oval negative spaces. These spaces,
or panels, are filled with ornamental
elements, sometimes representing
ghost elbows and fingers, or
stylizations of the praying mantis. The
ground may be filled with red
pigment, against which the relief
design stands out clearly; paint does
not adhere to the glossy, bamboo
surface of the relief itself. Decoration
of a bamboo blowing horn could be
done in just a few days. Originally
stone axes, animals' teeth and shells
were the Asmat's only tools for
carving.

65. Bride Price

Bismarck Ranges, Papua New Guinea
Tridacna shell
14 cm x 13 cm
c. 1930
Collection: James Davidson

66. Antique Comb

Bali, Indonesia
Wood carved with intricate floral
motifs and meanders
25 cm x 6.3 cm
Early 20th century
Collection: James Davidson

- Foods that are low in both kcalories and essential nutrients: coffee, tea, broth, some artificially sweetened products such as diet soft drinks and diet gelatin desserts, condiments

Using the food group information

Tables 10.2 and 10.3 summarize information about how many servings of foods from the four basic groups are needed by healthy people each day. They give recommendations for people of various ages, conditions, and lifestyles, such as pregnant and lactating women, athletes, vegetarians, and people on a tight budget.

Once you know the Basic Food Guide groups, serving sizes, and recommended minimum numbers of servings that apply to you, you can use this information to help yourself make more nutritious food selections. For example, if you customarily eat more than ten servings of grain products daily but only two or three servings of fruits and vegetables, the Basic Food Guide recommendations suggest that you might substitute a piece of fresh fruit as a snack instead of your usual package of cheese crackers. Or when you arrive at the cafeteria for supper, you can mentally tally up what you have eaten so far that day, and quickly use the Basic Food Guide to decide what items will fulfill your remaining needs for the day.

Table 10.2   Basic food guide recommendations for various ages and reproductive statuses

	Include at least this many servings daily				
	Child ½–9 years	Child 9–12 years	Teen[a]	Adult[a]	Pregnant or lactating
Fruits and vegetables [b]					
Vitamin A rich	1	1	1	1	1
Vitamin C rich	1	1	1	1	2
Others	2	2	2	2	2
Total	4	4	4	4	5
Grain products (preferably whole grain; otherwise enriched or fortified)	4[c]	4	4	4	4 or more for adequate weight gain
Milk and milk products	2–3	3	4	2	4[e]
Meats and alternates	2[d]	2	2	2	3

[a]A *teen* is defined as a person who has added height in the past year and is at least 12 years old; an *adult* has not added height in that time.
[b]For preschool children, serving size is 1 tablespoon per year of age.
[c]Give smaller servings, depending on age.
[d]For preschool children, serving size is half of the standard serving.
[e]For pregnant teenagers, increase to 5 servings.

Table 10.3   Basic food guide recommendations for certain lifestyles

| | Include at least this many servings daily | | | | |
| | Athletes | | Adult vegetarians | | |
	Teen	Adult	Who use milk	Who use only plant foods	Adults with limited budget
Fruits and vegetables	Fruits/vegetables: 1 vitamin A 1 vitamin C Others to make group total of 4		Fruits:1–4, including 1 raw vitamin C Vegetables: 3, including 1 or more dark leafy green	Fruits:1–4, including 1 raw vitamin C Vegetables: 4, including 2 or more dark leafy green	Fruits/vegetables: 1 vitamin A 1 vitamin C Others to make group total of 4
Grain products	4–12 or more as needed for energy		Whole grain yeast bread: 3 slices Other grains: 2	Whole grain yeast bread: 4 slices Other grains: 3–5	9–12
Milk and milk products	4 (teen) 2 (adult)		2	0	1½
Meats and alternates	2		Legumes: 1 serving Nuts or seeds: ½ serving	Nuts or seeds: 1 serving { Fortified soybean milk: 2 cups Legumes: ⅓ cup } or { Legumes: 1¼ cup Good sources of vitamin B-12[a] and calcium[b] }	2

[a]Good sources of vitamin B-12 are: fortified soy milk, fortified nutritional yeast, vitamin supplement (Robertson, 1976).
[b]Good sources of calcium are: fortified soy milk, some leafy greens, sunflower seeds, unhulled sesame seeds, blackstrap molasses (Robertson, 1976).

Using the rulers

Here are examples of how to use the rulers to monitor and modify your intakes of fat, sodium, and added sugar.

Let's say that when you assessed what proportions of your energy intake came from protein, fat, and carbohydrate (as described in Chapter 9), you learned that you consumed too much fat.

One approach to lowering your fat consumption would be to look at the fat rulers in Figures 10.1 through 10.6 to see what levels of fat are in the foods you consumed. Look at the limited extras first: are you eating many that are high in fat? If so, it would make good sense to

For most people, supplementation is not necessary, but there are some special situations in which it is useful. In this section we will describe when it is and when it is not needed.

Why people take supplements

This section lists some reasons people give for taking supplements. We have grouped them according to how justifiable supplementation is on scientific grounds.

Definitely needed:

- People who eat no animal products (vegans) need vitamin B-12 supplementation; they may also benefit from supplements of vitamin D, riboflavin, calcium, iron, and/or zinc if intakes are low.

  Often useful:

- The following age-groups of people, even if they seem to eat sensibly, often benefit from a multiple vitamin and mineral supplement: babies; all women in childbearing years (iron is the main concern here), but especially pregnant and lactating women; and elderly people.
- Weight-reduction dieters and very inactive people may benefit from a vitamin and mineral supplement, since kcaloric restriction often results in lower intakes of micronutrients.
- People undergoing physical stress, such as an illness, accident, or surgery, may benefit from a vitamin and mineral supplement since needs are higher at such times.

  Useful in selected cases:

- People with *severe* acne usually benefit from taking oral 13-cis-retinoic acid, a synthetic form of vitamin A. It is available only by prescription, since it can have dangerous side effects.
- Chronic users of medication may benefit from a supplement, depending on the drugs and dosages involved. For example, a small proportion of women who take oral contraceptive agents become depleted in vitamin B-6 and therefore benefit from supplementation. However, most do not need it. Check with your health care provider if you are on any ongoing medication.
- Chronic alcohol users may benefit from a general vitamin supplement, since vitamins (especially B vitamins) are depleted during the metabolism of alcohol. However, such supplements do nothing to allay the direct toxic effects of alcohol.

  Questionable:

- Prevention of colds. Although inadequate intake of vitamin C results in poor immune function, supplments above the RDA level do not significantly reduce the incidence of colds; massive doses of vitamin C actually interfere with immune function.

- Cure of colds. Several studies show that vitamin C supplements taken at the start of a cold reduce the severity of symptoms and result in an average of a half day less at home. However, since there are risks from high intakes of vitamin C, a mild antihistamine is the preferred therapy for this purpose.
- Cancer prevention. Although *diets* high in vitamins A and C are associated with lower cancer incidence, the vitamins themselves may not be the reason; other substances in the food might be responsible. For now, it appears better to eat *foods* high in these vitamins.
- Enhanced athletic ability. Supplements above RDA levels have no benefit.
- Relief from emotional stress. There is no evidence that *emotional* stress increases the need for micronutrients, although *physical* stress does (as mentioned under the "often useful" heading).
- Relief from premenstrual syndrome (PMS). Although various self-styled PMS therapists recommend large micronutrient supplements, current evidence does not support the safety or effectiveness of such "therapy."

Guidelines for safe supplementation

Healthy people who want to take a general nutritional supplement (even though it may not be necessary to do so) can get maximal benefit with minimal risk by following these suggestions:

- Limit yourself to supplements that provide no more than 150 percent of the U.S. RDA. Different formulations vary considerably in how potent they are; protect yourself against overdosing.
- Use multinutrient formulations, so that nutrient intakes are fairly well balanced.
- Examine expiration dates on containers; vitamins gradually deteriorate with time.
- Consider cost. "Natural" vitamins are usually more expensive than synthetic versions, but are not more effective.
- Eat a well-balanced diet anyway. There is no pill that provides all of the approximately 50 essential nutrients.

Food for Athletes

Dedicated athletes look for every possible way to improve performance. They train faithfully, trying with each workout to push themselves a little beyond what they achieved before. Being highly motivated—"psyched up"—also helps, and athletes also know that good nutrition can make a difference.

There is no question that good general nutrition, such as we have discussed with the Basic Food Guide, is important for any athlete's physical well-being and performance. Getting 10 to 15 percent of kcalories from protein, up to 30 percent from fat, and 50 to 60 percent from carbohydrate is healthy for the athlete, just as it is for everybody else. However, endurance athletes may realize performance benefits from routinely getting 60 to 65 percent of their kcalories from carbohydrates (and decreasing their fat intake).

But beyond that, how can nutrition offer a competitive edge?

More water

As emphasized in Chapters 6 and 8, when water levels decrease by approximately 3 percent of body weight, physical performance begins to deteriorate; greater losses result in increasingly severe performance penalties. For this reason, water is the nutrient that the athlete needs to consume in the largest extra quantities. (Because we discussed this topic in detail earlier, here we have given only this brief reminder of water's primary importance.)

Extra energy from more carbohydrate

Athletes of all kinds, but endurance athletes in particular, require more kcalories. How many extra kcalories they need depends on the particular sport, how long they do it, and their body weight. Table 10.6 will give you an idea of how much energy is expended in various sports. (Table 4.9 gave values in METS for some activities.)

The athlete's daily diet—high carbohydrate   The best way to get the extra kcalories an athlete needs is to consume more foods that are high in carbohydrate. Grain products, fruits, and vegetables—especially legumes—are good sources. The Basic Food Guide recommends 4 to 12 or more servings of grain products for athletes; with each serving providing 70 to 100 kcalories, ten additional servings provide almost 1000 more kcalories.

The reason that extra carbohydrate is recommended is that the body readily utilizes carbohydrate for energy. Furthermore, carbohydrate refills the body's stores of glycogen; this is important because physical endurance is directly related to the amount of glycogen in the muscles involved (Figure 10.7).

The person who gets 50 to 60 percent of his or her energy from carbohydrate maintains sufficient levels of glycogen for at least one and a half hours of vigorous, nonstop aerobic activity per day. This is adequate for the training and competing needs of many athletes. Those who train much longer may benefit from 60 to 65 percent of kcalories from carbohydrate.

Table 10.6 How to burn it: Amount of energy used during one hour of activity

Activity	Energy used (kcal)	
	205-lb person	125-lb person
Archery	420	268
Baseball—infield or outfield	382	234
—pitching	488	299
Basketball—moderate	575	352
—vigorous	807	495
Bicycling—on level, 5.5 mph	409	251
13.0 mph	877	537
Canoeing—4 mph	565	352
Dancing—moderate	341	209
—vigorous	464	284
Fencing—moderate	409	251
—vigorous	837	513
Football	678	416
Golf—twosome	443	271
—foursome	332	203
Handball or hardball—vigorous	797	488
Horseback riding—walk	270	165
—trot	551	338
Motorcycling	297	182
Mountain climbing	820	503
Rowing—pleasure	409	251
—rowing machine or sculling, 20 strokes/min	1116	684
Running—5.5 mph	887	537
—7 mph	1141	669
—9 mph level	1269	777
—9 mph, 2.5% grade	1480	907
—9 mph, 4% grade	1564	959
—12 mph	1606	984
—in place, 140 count/min	1993	1222
Skating—moderate	465	285
—vigorous	837	513
Skiing—downhill	789	483
—level, 5 mph	956	586
Soccer	730	447
Squash	849	520
Swimming—backstroke, 20 yds/min	316	194
40 yds/min	682	418
—breaststroke, 20 yds/min	392	241
40 yds/min	786	482
—butterfly	956	586
—crawl, 20 yds/min	392	241
50 yds/min	869	532
—sidestroke	682	418

(Continued)

Table 10.6   (Continued)

Activity	Energy used (kcal)	
	205-lb person	125-lb person
Tennis—moderate	565	347
—vigorous	797	488
Volleyball—moderate	465	285
—vigorous	797	489
Walking—2 mph	286	176
—110–120 paces/min	425	260
—4.5 mph	540	331
—downstairs	544	333
—upstairs	1417	869
Water skiing	638	391
Wrestling, judo, or karate	1049	643

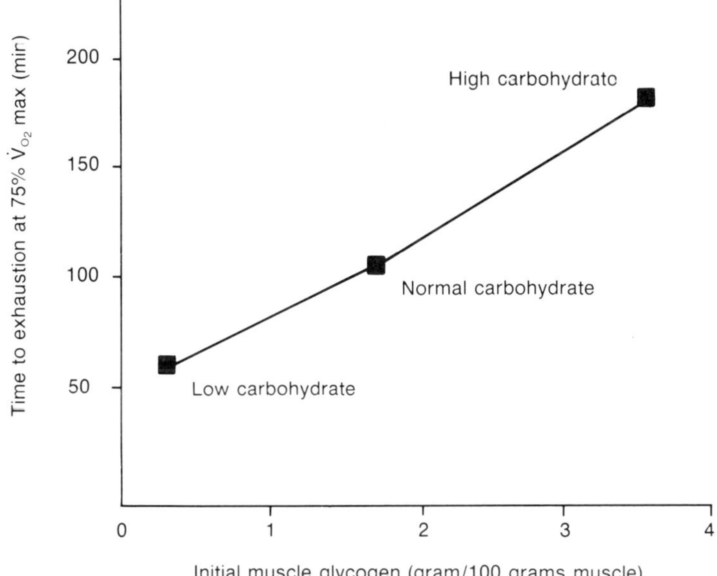

Figure 10.7   Carbohydrate for the long haul. The proportion of carbohydrate in your diet affects the amount stored in your body in the form of glycogen, which in turn affects your endurance.

Carbohydrate loading for occasional use   People who exercise strenuously and continuously for more than one and a half hours at a time are at risk of depleting their body glycogen stores. Trained distance runners describe this as "hitting the wall," which is most likely to happen after about 22 miles of running. To avoid this, endurance athletes may benefit from increasing their store of glycogen before long-distance competition. The routine for doing this is usually called **car-**

Carbohydrate loading: An exercise and diet regimen that leads to increased storage of glycogen.

bohydrate loading (or less commonly, *glycogen loading* or *glycogen supercompensation*).

This process begins about a week before the event, and has both exercise and dietary aspects. Early versions consisted of a far more rigorous regimen than the routine recommended in 1986 by the noted exercise physiologist David Costill in his book titled *Inside Running*. Costill's recommendations for the runner are given below, but could be adapted easily for other distance events:

- Exercise—starting one week before the event, reduce training intensity. In the 48 to 72 hours before competition, limit training to a daily warmup of one to three easy miles.
- Food consumption—on the sixth, fifth, and fourth days before the event, eat a normal diet. Then in the days immediately before the event, consume a very high carbohydrate diet, with approximately 70 percent of the kcalories from carbohydrate (up from the amount recommended for usual intake).

This results in a substantial increase of glycogen level in the muscles involved.

Table 10.7 gives an example of a 3000-kcalorie diet that derives 70 to 75 percent of its energy from carbohydrate. Notice how very low in fat and moderate in protein this diet is: no butter or mayonnaise on the sandwich or French bread, skim milk rather than 2 percent or whole milk, and no meat in the spaghetti sauce. Although this diet reaches the intended carbohydrate level, it does not meet recommended intakes of all other nutrients; therefore it should not be used in this extreme a version for more than a few days at a time.

Not everybody likes the way his or her body feels after carbohydrate loading. This is because extra water is retained in the muscles along with the glycogen. This can produce feelings of stiffness and heaviness, and may interfere with performance in some athletes. (With the earlier regimens, a few even experienced chest discomfort and temporary abnormalities in heart function.) Therefore if you want to try carbohydrate loading, do not do it for the first time just before competing; try it out at some other time, so that if you don't like the way you feel from it, you haven't risked your participation in the upcoming event.

When NOT to use carbohydrate   With so much emphasis on the positive aspects of carbohydrate for the endurance athlete, you may think that it is always beneficial. However, this is not true: a high carbohydrate intake just before exercise can have a negative effect. If a person drinks a large amount of sugar solution (the amount of sugar in two 12-ounce cans of regular carbonated beverage) 30 to 60 minutes before starting endurance activity, he or she becomes exhausted sooner than if plain water had been consumed (Costill, 1982).

Table 10.7   Carbohydrate-loader's cuisine: a 3000-kcalorie diet that provides 70–75% of its kcalories as carbohydrate.

Breakfast
8 oz. orange juice
½ cup Grape-nuts
1 medium banana
8 oz. skim milk
1 whole-wheat English muffin
1 tablespoon jelly

Lunch
2 sandwiches:
   4 slices bread
   4 oz. sliced white meat of turkey
   lettuce and tomato
1 cup orange sherbet
8 oz. skim milk

Dinner
1½ cups cooked spaghetti noodles
   (3 oz. before cooking)
1/2 cup tomato sauce with mushrooms
2 tablespoons Parmesan cheese
4 slices French bread
1 cup cooked green peas (from frozen)
½ cup applesauce
8 oz. skim milk

Snacks
¼ cup raisins
8 oz. apple juice
1 cup chocolate ice milk

This occurs because a large dose of carbohydrate stimulates increased production of the hormone insulin; this, in turn, causes sugar to be taken up by the body cells quickly and put into storage instead of remaining readily available for energy production. The increased insulin also interferes with the body's use of fat for energy. To avoid this, consume your carbohydrates *several hours* before you begin activity. After a couple of hours, your body will be metabolically geared to expending more energy.

Carbohydrate DURING endurance activity   During endurance activities lasting more than 90 minutes, it may be useful to drink a sugar solution as a hedge against glycogen depletion. However, if you use enough sugar to provide much extra energy, the high concentration of sugar may delay stomach emptying and postpone the benefits of the sugar and water. For this reason, athletes should not consume beverages containing more than 10 percent sugar by weight during activity.

Protein needs   The major function of dietary protein for both the athlete and nonathlete is to provide the raw materials for repairing worn-out lean body tissue and constructing new tissue. Protein is *not a major energy source* for either the athlete or the nonathlete.

Recall that for the full-grown nonathlete, 0.8 grams of protein per kilogram of body weight per day meets these needs.

But what about the athlete? Is it possible that hard training and competition cause tissue damage that calls for more protein for repair? Does the weight lifter who is increasing muscle mass need extra protein to produce the additional tissue? Does the endurance athlete ever need to draw on protein in larger-than-usual amounts to complete a grueling long-distance event?

Research done within the last few years has shown that any of the above circumstances can increase the athlete's need for protein, but not by a very large amount. Considering all of these factors, exercise physiologists and nutritionists usually recommend protein intakes of approximately 1 gram/kg/day, which generally meet the athlete's needs. These are levels of protein intake that most people typically consume. Since this is so easy to achieve, protein supplements are unnecessary.

Because we know that many athletes have been steeped in a sports tradition that promotes protein intakes far beyond what is scientifically supportable, we believe many athletes consume far more protein than is necessary. This is of concern because at levels of more than 2 grams/kg/day, it is possible that negative consequences will occur—such as dehydration, calcium loss, and excessive fat intake.

Vitamin needs

Although the need for some B vitamins increases with high energy intakes, normal food sources can supply them. Since athletes need more energy, with the extra food they eat they also get more vitamins—provided they do not rely on the nutrient-poor limited extras for most of their extra kcalories. Therefore vitamin supplements are not needed by most athletes.

Mineral needs

Needs for most minerals are not significantly greater for the athlete, although there are a few concerns.

Adequate iron is important for the athlete. Iron is a necessary component of the blood protein hemoglobin, which carries oxygen to body tissues. If iron and therefore hemoglobin is low (as in iron-deficiency anemia), energy metabolism is compromised and physical performance suffers. Therefore athletes need to keep their iron and hemoglobin levels within the normal range.

Iron-deficiency anemia is more of a risk for female than for male athletes, because women's needs for iron are higher due to menstrual losses. Therefore, female athletes especially should have an annual blood test for iron status. The RDA for men is 10 mg of iron; for women it is 18 mg of iron. Poor iron status can often be improved by eating more foods that are good iron sources (Table 10.8). Remember that you can improve the bioavailability of iron in plant sources by including some meat, fish, or poultry or a good source of vitamin C at the same meal.

People who have just begun a rigorous physical training program sometimes develop low levels of hemoglobin. For the first few weeks of their program, they may experience anemia; however, it is usually temporary, and hemoglobin levels return to normal within a few weeks. There is no need to treat this anemia, since it will resolve itself shortly.

Another concern many athletes have is that they will suffer from the loss of other body minerals in sweat. For most athletes, this concern is unnecessary, as will be explained below. (Possible exceptions would be people who participate in events of more than seven hours, such as ultramarathons and triathlons.)

The two main minerals lost in sweat are sodium and chloride. Since the body usually contains more of both of them than is needed, there is little reason for most athletes to worry about them. Furthermore, when you sweat, you lose proportionately more water than minerals, so the mineral component in your body becomes increasingly concentrated. Therefore the most critical need is rehydration. After that is begun, you can easily restore sodium and chloride by including a salty food at the next meal. The sodium rulers of the Basic Food Guide can help you choose.

Salt tablets should be avoided because they are irritating to the GI tract, can increase the danger of dehydration, and may cause diarrhea which further contributes to dehydration.

As far as other minerals, such as potassium, are concerned, don't worry. Although you lose some in sweat, your body generally conserves such minerals by reducing their excretion rate by the kidneys.

The pre-event meal

Most of the nutrients a person uses for energy during exercise were taken in at least several hours or even days before. You do not need to eat just before exercising in order to have energy; in fact, your last meal should be *at least three hours before the event*. If you eat a lot just before activity, it is likely to hinder performance rather than help. The next paragraphs explain why.

For a couple of hours after you have eaten, a large portion of your blood supply concentrates in the intestinal region to be ready to transport absorbed nutrients. If you are physically active at the same time,

Table 10.8 Iron content of some foods

Food	Amount	Iron (mg)
		0 2 4 6 8
Fruits and vegetables		
Apricots, raw	2–3 medium	x[a]
Apricots, dried	3 large halves	xx
Beans, green snap, cooked	½ c	x
Broccoli, chopped, cooked	½ c	x
Corn, cooked	½ c	x
Lettuce, iceberg	⅙ head	x
Orange juice	½ c	
Peas, green, cooked	½ c	xxx
Potatoes, mashed with milk	½ c	x
Raisins	2 T	x
Spinach, chopped, cooked	½ c	xxxx
Turnip greens, cooked	½ c	xxx
Grain products		
Bread, whole grain	1 slice	xx
Bread, white enriched	1 slice	x
Bread, unenriched	1 slice	
Cereal, bran flakes	1 oz	xxxxxxxxx
Cereal, wheat flakes, iron-fortified	1 oz	xxxxxxxxx
Cereal, shredded wheat	1 oz	xx
Spaghetti, enriched	½ c	x
Milk and milk products		
Milk	1 c	
Cheese, cheddar	1⅓ oz	x
Meat and alternates		
Almonds	½ c	xxxxxx
Beans, canned with tomato sauce and pork	1 c	xxxxxxxxx
Beef, ground, broiled	3 oz	xxxxxx
Chicken breast, cooked	3 oz	xxx
Eggs, hard boiled	2	xxxx
Liver, beef, cooked	3 oz	xxxxxxxxxxxxxxxx
Peanut butter	¼ c	xx
Shrimp, canned	3 oz	xxxxx
Tuna, canned	3 oz	xxx
Walnuts, chopped	½ c	xxxx
Limited extras		
Beer	12 oz	
Butter, margarine	1 t	
Carbonated beverages	12 oz	
Honey	1 T	
Molasses, light	1 T	xx
Sugar, white	1 T	

[a]Each "x" represents 0.5 mg of iron.

For a couple of hours after you have eaten, a large portion of your blood supply concentrates in the intestinal region to be ready to transport absorbed nutrients. If you are physically active at the same time, your muscles simultaneously need a larger volume of blood. Neither area can have the optimal amount, so neither function can work as well as it might.

Furthermore, when a person is going to compete, tension or pregame stress can influence how his or her body handles food. Tension can decrease blood flow to the stomach and small intestine, delay the digestion and absorption of food, cause nausea and vomiting, or increase the activity of the lower intestinal tract resulting in diarrhea. These possible consequences are more good reasons for not eating within a few hours of competing.

What should the pregame meal consist of? It should contain foods the athlete likes and has always tolerated well. Another useful guideline is to limit the meal to small or moderate size; 500 to 1000 kcalories is reasonable. It will be digested and absorbed more quickly if it is low in fat, moderate in protein, and high in carbohydrate.

Commercial liquid pregame meals are an alternative to eating solid foods. Generally, these products offer the advantages of having low volume while being nourishing, convenient, and relatively quick to leave the stomach. Athletes who like the taste of these products usually find them very satisfactory. They can be especially useful for tournament days when intermittent activity throughout the day makes energy intake necessary but there is no time for regular meals.

In this chapter, we have shown how the Basic Food Guide can be used by people of all ages and levels of physical activity for choosing a healthy diet. Good food-handling practices can also bring you closer to your goal of good nutrition. For a few groups of people, nutrient supplementation is in order.

In addition, we've considered special nutritional needs of dedicated athletes, emphasizing water and carbohydrate needs. No fancy liquids, powders, or secret ingredients are necessary—just eat a varied diet of ordinary foods, train well, and step up to the starting line.

Weight Control: Of Lifetime Value

11

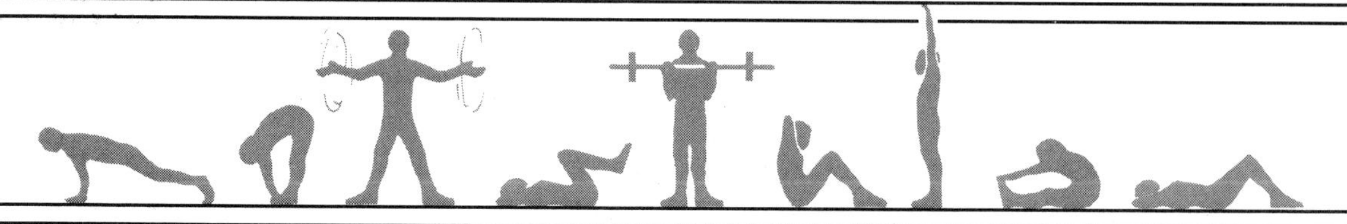

Outline

Many people are dissatisfied with their body weight. This is evident in that Americans spend billions of dollars annually on products and services to change—usually decrease—body weight. At last count, over 30,000 different methods have been marketed for weight control.

Weight control *should* be of concern to people: overweight is associated with many diseases that interfere with enjoyment of living. It can also shorten life. Since approximately one-third of adult Americans and up to one-fifth of our children are overweight, a lot of lives are being lived less fully because of excess body weight.

But let's be honest. Improving health is not the main reason most people try to lose weight; appearance is. Today there is tremendous social pressure to be thin. If you compare beauty contest winners over the last several decades, you will see that our culture's concept of the body beautiful has been getting progressively thinner. Women, especially, feel pressure in this regard.

Whatever people's reasons have been for trying to lose weight, the methods they have used apparently haven't worked very well. After all, if any existing products or services *really worked*, there wouldn't be a market for hundreds of other solutions.

Oddly enough, at the same time that there are many overweight Americans, there are also some people in our population who are dangerously underweight—especially teenage girls and young women with anorexia nervosa. They are at risk of actually killing themselves by becoming too thin.

How strange all of this concern with weight is, considering that in the rest of the animal kingdom individuals generally maintain a stable weight throughout adult life, provided there is an adequate food supply. Some animals are larger or smaller than average, of course, but they tend to have appropriate amounts of fat for their size.

Such thoughts prompt a variety of questions. If other animals do it so effortlessly, why do human beings have to struggle so hard to achieve and/or maintain the "right" weight? And just what is ideal weight? How can a person get there and stay there?

In this chapter, we will draw upon the current thinking in nutrition, sports physiology, and psychology to answer such questions.

Why Are Human Beings Different?

Why is it that we don't automatically regulate our weight (technically, our amount of body fat) at appropriate levels like other animals do?

After all, our bodies—just like those of other animals—are naturally equipped to make us hungry enough to replace the kcalories we have expended, and then to feel satisfied when we have eaten enough. These mechanisms are tuned to produce energy balance and stable weight (stable amount of body fat). But unlike other animals, we often override the inborn mechanisms that control energy balance.

People are influenced by additional factors on both the intake and output sides of the energy balance equation. On the intake side, we may eat simply because food is handy, or because it is urged on us in a social situation; because it is a certain time of day; because we are bored; or because it makes us feel better emotionally. We might avoid eating if we are tired or stressed, we don't have time, we are short of cash, or because we are trying to lose weight. The factors that cause people to eat or not eat are quite individual.

As far as output is concerned, we are not as spontaneously active as most animals. In the wild, animals need to expend energy to find food everytime they want to eat. Many people, on the other hand, can eat regularly without being very physically active to obtain their food; sedentary lifestyles are common.

With so many factors that can affect energy intake and output besides the inborn regulators, it is not surprising that people may have trouble maintaining energy balance, and therefore a consistent, appropriate body weight.

Why Be Concerned about Weight?

As far as health is concerned, there is a great deal of evidence that being very overweight or very underweight puts a person at risk of early death. But even if death does not occur prematurely, there are other penalties for people at either extreme of the weight spectrum.

An *extremely underweight* individual has lower physical strength and endurance, lessened resistance to infectious diseases, and (in women) decreased ability to reproduce. People who are very underweight are also more likely to have nutritional deficiency diseases, and do not have a sense of well-being.

Being *overweight*, on the other hand, increases a person's risk of atherosclerosis (a cardiovascular problem which will be discussed in the next chapter), high blood pressure, certain types of cancer, diabetes, gallbladder disease, arthritis, gout, skin disorders, kidney and upper respiratory problems, accident-proneness, surgical complications, and (in women) disorders of the reproductive system.

As far as social effects are concerned, being substantially overweight can jeopardize a person's occupational and social success. Although there are laws that prohibit overt discrimination against overweight people in screening applicants for school entrance and job openings, discrimination still exists in many informal ways; just ask any obese person. Even children of preschool age often have negative attitudes toward fat peers.

One consequence of these attitudes is that the overweight person often develops a poor self-concept, which adds to his or her difficulties. The more overweight a person is, the greater the magnitude of the associated problems.

What Should You Weigh?

Before going any further, we need to define some terms: **overweight**, as used in scientific papers, usually means 10 to 20 percent above ideal body weight; **obese** means more than 20 percent above the ideal. The term **ideal (or best) body weight** is much more difficult to define, as this section will demonstrate.

Overweight: Between 10 percent and 20 percent above ideal body weight.

Obese: In excess of 20 percent above ideal body weight.

Ideal body weight: A person's most appropriate weight, based on a combination of statistical and individual factors.

Standards for assessing body weight

In this section we will discuss some standards commonly used to evaluate body weight, and we will be very blunt about their limitations:

there is no perfect standard to determine your ideal weight. Rather, the most realistic approach is to measure yourself against several of the standards described below—the height/weight table, skinfold measurements, and your perceived set-point—and combine their results to decide what you should weigh.

The cultural standard—what our society thinks is beautiful—offers poor guidance, especially for women. We'll discuss this issue first, and then go on to more useful concepts.

Cultural influences   Every culture has some vision of the body beautiful, and one aspect of that vision is weight. How these attitudes are formed is a complex matter, involving not only aesthetics, but economic and, more recently, health considerations as well. For example, in some very poor societies it is considered desirable to be fat because it demonstrates the relative wealth of the person who can afford enough food to become overweight. In other cultures, a fat woman is regarded as content.

These beliefs are distinctly different from the current North American attitude that prizes extreme leanness. Such cultural pressure has influenced most women to believe that they are too fat, no matter what their current weight is; even many who are at an acceptable body weight from a health perspective believe they ought to lose weight.

Our culture puts less pressure on men to be thin; it generally sanctions weights that they can maintain quite easily and comfortably. Therefore, men are much more realistic about what body weight is appropriate for them.

Some popular literature suggests that the best way to assess whether you are overweight is to spend a few moments of naked truth in front of a full-length mirror. We doubt that most people—again, especially women—could *correctly* assess their best weight in this manner.

To summarize this topic: at present, our culture often pressures women to try to be thinner than is healthy for them.

The standards that follow offer healthier—although still less than perfect—guidance.

Height and weight data   For decades, the weight standards most familiar to Americans have been the tables published by the Metropolitan Insurance Company, as shown in Tables 11.1 and 11.2. Table 11.1 suggests appropriate weight ranges based on sex, height, and body frame size. Table 11.2 helps you determine your body frame size. Table 11.1 was developed to show the weights that people who lived the longest were at ages 25 to 59.

Although such height/weight tables have been widely accepted as authoritative, there are many reasons that they should be regarded as *general guidelines rather than rigid recommendations*.

For one thing, weight data do not always accurately reflect how fat a person is. This is significant, since it is probably body fat, rather than

Table 11.1 Metropolitan height and weight tables[a]

Height	Weight (lb)		
	Small frame	Medium frame	Large frame
Men			
5'1"	123–129	126–136	133–145
5'2"	125–131	128–138	135–148
5'3"	127–133	130–140	137–151
5'4"	129–135	132–143	139–155
5'5"	131–137	134–146	141–159
5'6"	133–140	137–149	144–163
5'7"	135–143	140–152	147–167
5'8"	137–146	143–155	150–171
5'9"	139–149	146–158	153–175
5'10"	141–152	149–161	156–179
5'11"	144–155	152–165	159–183
6'	147–159	155–169	163–187
6'1"	150–163	159–173	167–192
6'2"	153–167	162–177	171–197
6'3"	157–171	166–182	176–202
Women			
4'9"	98–108	106–118	115–128
4'10"	100–110	108–120	117–131
4'11"	101–112	110–123	119–134
5'	103–115	112–126	122–137
5'1"	105–118	115–129	125–140
5'2"	108–121	118–132	128–144
5'3"	111–124	121–135	131–148
5'4"	114–127	124–138	134–152
5'5"	117–130	127–141	137–156
5'6'	120–133	130–144	140–160
5'7"	123–136	133–147	143–164
5'8"	126–139	136–150	146–167
5'9"	129–142	139–153	149–170
5'10"	132–145	142–156	152–173
5'11"	133–148	145–159	155–176

[a]Weights at ages 25 to 59 based on lowest mortality; height measured without shoes and weight without clothes.

weight per se, that is the real health issue. A dedicated athlete who has developed a large muscle mass may exceed the recommended weight range but have very little body fat. An older person may have lost considerable muscle mass through inactivity and may be within the recommended weight range but be overly fat.

In addition, many questions have been raised regarding the quality of the statistics used in generating these tables (such as, when were weights taken, and how?) and the way the data were handled (such

Table 11.2 Determining frame size from elbow breadth

To determine your frame size, extend your arm and bend the forearm upward at a 90 degree angle. Keep the fingers straight and turn the inside of your wrist away from your body. Place the thumb and index finger of your other hand on the two prominent bones on *either side* of your elbow. Measure the space between your fingers against a ruler or a tape measure.[a] Compare the measurements on the following tables.

These tables list the elbow measurements for medium-framed men and women of various heights. Measurements lower than those listed indicate that you have a small frame, and higher measurements indicate a large frame.

Height	Elbow breadth (inches)
Men	
5'1"–5'2"	2½"–2⅞"
5'3"–5'6"	2⅝"–2⅞"
5'7"–5'10"	2¾"–3"
5'11"–6'2"	2¾"–3⅛"
6'3"	2⅞"–3¼"
Women	
4'9"–4'10"	2¼"–2½"
4'11"–5'2"	2¼"–2½"
5'3"–5'6"	2⅜"–2⅝"
5'7"–5'10"	2⅜"–2⅝"
5'11"	2½"–2¾"

[a]For the most accurate measurement, measure your elbow breadth with a caliper.

as, was the effect of smoking on longevity separated from the effect of weight?).

Nevertheless, despite their flaws, height/weight tables suggest weight ranges that are reasonable general guidelines for "average" adults.

Percentage of body fat   Because excess body fat is probably the real culprit, several methods have been developed to measure body fat more directly. The most accurate techniques are potassium measurement and underwater weighing, methods that require specialized research equipment. From such techniques, physiologists have determined the percentage of body weight that is fat in the "typical" man and woman. Based on his review of the literature, one expert says it is typical for a man to have 15 percent fat, and for a woman to have 27 percent fat (Lohman, 1981). Another suggests normal ranges of 12 to 16 percent for men, and 22 to 26 percent for women (Williams, 1985). These data apply to the general population but not to athletes, whose percentage of body fat is likely to be lower.

Of course, most people will never have the opportunity to be assessed by these methods. They may, however, have access to a more available but less accurate method—skinfold measurement. With this technique, the thickness of the fat layer beneath the skin at various body sites is measured, and then tables are used to convert the measurements into body fat percentages.

But just as the height/weight tables are subject to certain inaccuracies, so is skinfold testing. Variation in results can occur due to the calipers being inaccurate, the technique of the person doing the measurement, the number of body sites measured, the choice of sites, and the tables used for conversion. Therefore, like height/weight tables, skinfold measurements fall short of being the "gold standard" for ideal body weight.

Nonetheless, skinfold measurements have value: *in practiced hands*, these measurements can provide a reasonable estimate of overall body fatness. If repeated at intervals over several weeks or months, they can also show whether body fat is increasing or decreasing. This can be particularly useful for someone who is trying to lose fat by both dieting and exercising; the person's body weight may not be changing at all, but fat may be decreasing while muscle is being added. Without skinfold testing, the person whose weight is not decreasing might think, "My program's not working," and abandon what might actually be a very successful *fat* loss method.

Similarly, skinfold measurements can be used to compare the fatness of different groups of people. For example, in Figure 11.1 the skinfold thickness of men of high, intermediate, and low activity levels are compared. The data in this figure reveal two interesting points: the most active people had the least body fat; and the fattest people in this study consumed the fewest kcalories per kilogram of body weight.

Note: We have emphasized that in order to get reliable values the person who measures skinfolds must be an expert; this is why we have not given instructions here for using the technique yourself. Rather, seek out an exercise physiologist, coach, trainer, dietitian, or physician who routinely does skinfold measurement.

Set-point levels   Some psychologists have suggested that a new factor, called the **set-point**, may be important. The set-point theory suggests that each person has a particular weight that he or she tends to maintain, and at which the body functions in a metabolically normal way; this is referred to as the person's set-point. It has been likened to a thermostat: although people may temporarily gain or lose weight by deliberate changes in food intake, they will return to their set-points after they resume eating in response to hunger (Keesey and Corbett, 1984). In terms of the set-point theory, your ideal body weight is the weight you maintain when you get adequate *exercise*, eat in response to true *hunger*, and stop eating when *satisfied*. The only way to determine your set-point is to adopt these eating and exercise habits and see what weight you attain and maintain.

People who are overweight may welcome this theory as an explanation for their predicament, but may at the same time feel trapped

Set-point: The weight at which a person's body functions in a metabolically normal way; the weight a person returns to after a forced gain or loss of weight.

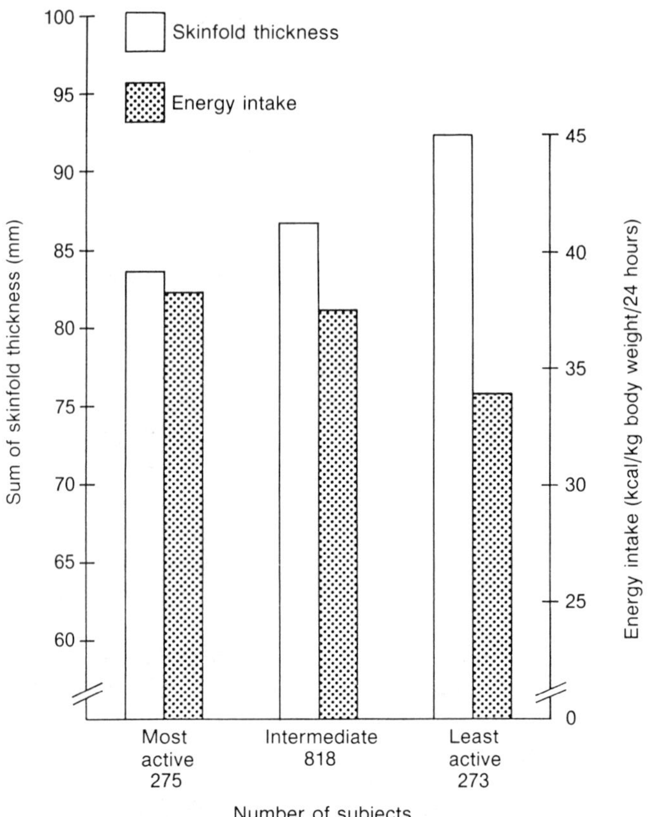

Figure 11.1 Comparison of skinfold thickness and kcalorie intake between groups of men of different activity levels.

by it at their current body weights. This need not necessarily be the case, as the next few paragraphs explain.

Exercise seems to play a role in determining a person's set-point. A person who is very inactive physically may have a higher set-point—that is, weigh more—than he or she would with more activity. If an inactive person increases activity to moderate levels, his or her set-point is lowered, hunger decreases, and body weight will gradually and comfortably decrease.

Therefore this theory is not a universal cop-out, making your current weight acceptable, no matter what it is; rather, it demands that certain conditions be met—exercise moderately, eat only when hungry, stop when satisfied—before you can claim that your present weight is your set-point.

You can put it together

Chances are, you have already applied some of the above standards to yourself. You may have found that they don't all agree, even after you have discounted current cultural ideals. What can you do about disparate recommendations?

For example, you may have found that your present weight is somewhat above or below the range recommended by the height/weight table. Yet you may say, "This is the weight at which I function best and feel healthy. Whenever I lose (or gain) weight, it's only temporary, and I always return to this weight afterwards (i.e., it seems to be my set-point)." At the same time, you may have learned that your percentage of body fat is within the normal range when a dietitian or exercise leader tested you.

Should you try to change your weight? Or should you try to change your body fat, if your weight is normal but your body fat is not? Or should you try to change both, if both measurements were outside the recommended ranges?

That depends. Here's an example of a case in which it may not be advisable to try to make changes: if your nutrient intakes are fairly close to the RDAs (in other words, if you're being adequately but not excessively nourished), if you get at least a moderate amount of exercise, and if previous attempts to fit into the "right range" on the chart have not been successful, it is probably best for you to simply accept your current weight and get on with other aspects of living.

On the other hand, here are cases that call for action: if you are above your suggested weight range and seldom exercise, or frequently eat (or eat to excess) when you are not truly hungry, changes are in order. If you are below your range and eat erratically, changes are also in order. An artificially high or low body weight that results from unhealthy living habits cannot be justified and should be corrected.

Based on the standards we have discussed, some of you know that it would be in your best health interest to either lose or gain some weight. If you are one of those people, here we offer some guidelines for how to change and maintain body weight.

Our approach to weight control starts with the suggestion that you scrutinize both sides of your energy equation—both intake and output—to find out which of your present living habits may be keeping you from your best body weight, and why.

Once you have answered this question, you can determine how to modify your lifestyle to promote gradual weight change. Since one pound of body fat has the energy value of approximately 3500 kcalories, to lose a pound of fat you need to take in 3500 kcalories less than you expend, or—if you look at it from the other angle—expend 3500 kcalories more than you take in. Conversely, to gain a pound you must accumulate 3500 kcalories more than you expend.

You are most likely to have long-term success with maintaining a lower weight if you don't lose too much too fast. One to two pounds

Achieving and Maintaining Your Best Weight

per week is an attainable and maintainable goal. To lose one pound of body fat per week, you need to create an energy deficit of 500 kcalories per day; to lose two pounds, you have to expend 1000 more kcalories daily than you consume.

Studies of various weight-loss methods indicate that you are most likely to be successful at achieving weight change if you use behavior modification techniques (introduced in Chapter 2). In the following pages we will discuss how to apply these techniques. The specific examples we use will pertain to weight loss, since it interests more people than weight gain does. Gaining weight usually involves doing the opposite of what is recommended for losing weight.

Do not assume that you have to implement all the recommedations, or that many should be undertaken at once. As was pointed out in the earlier discussion of behavior modification, it is important to make lifestyle changes slowly. Since some people get such great pleasure from eating, if they try to change their habits too suddenly or too drastically, they become very uncomfortable and quickly give up the attempt.

Evaluating current behavior and planning changes

First, examine your eating habits, as described below.

Eating habits   Self-check 11.1 is a form you can use to record your eating habits: when, where, and what you ate; with whom you ate; what else you were doing; your emotional state and degree of hunger before you ate, and your feeling afterward—still hungry, satisfied, or "stuffed." Figure 11.2 is an example of a completed form.

After you have recorded your eating habits for one week, take a critical look at your filled-out form. First, analyze your diet using the Basic Food Guide. Food *quality* may be a problem: are many of the foods you eat high in fat, added sugar, or alcohol? Check your intake of limited extras, of foods within the four basic groups that are high in fat and sugar, and of alcoholic beverages. This could identify some of the sources of unnecessary kcalories, since a teaspoon of fat has 45 kcalories; a teaspoon of sugar, roughly 20; and an average serving of an alcoholic beverage, at least 100 kcalories. Note, however, the person who wants to *gain* weight should NOT consume more fat, sugar, and alcohol, because these substances can have negative effects on health. Consuming more complex carbohydrate and protein would be appropriate for such a person.

Food *quantity* might also be contributing to the problem. If you are an overweight person who consumed double or more than double the number of servings suggested by the minimums, you are probably consuming too much food. Did you really need this amount to feel satisfied, or did you feel "stuffed" after you ate?

Next, look at your negative eating habits as a behavioral psychologist would. Refer once again to Self-check 2.1 in Chapter 2 and use it to

Self-check 11.1 Recording your eating habits

Time		Place	Food and amount	Alone or with whom	Associated activity	Mood before eating	Hunger 0=none 5=intense	Feeling after eating
Enc	Start							

Figure 11.2   An example of an eating habits record (a filled-out form of Self-check 11.1).

Time		Place	Food and amount	Alone or with whom	Associated activity	Mood before eating	Hunger 0=none 5=intense	Feeling after eating
Start	End							
AM 8:10	8:15	kitchen	toasted bagel 4 oz. orange juice	alone	fixing lunch	neutral	2	satisfied
10:00	10:30	classroom	12 oz. cola	classmates	taking notes	busy	1	satisfied
PM 12:30	1:15	union cafeteria	1 sandwich 2 cookies 1 apple 1 carton 2% milk coffee	friends	talking	relaxed, happy	4	satisfied
4:30	4:45	apartment living room	12 snack crackers 12 oz. cola	alone	reading letter from friend	happy, unwinding	0	satisfied
7:30	7:50	restaurant	quarter pound cheeseburger medium order of fries strawberry shake	alone	reading magazine; taking break from studying	tense	2	stuffed
11:35	11:40	apartment living room	apple	alone	watching TV	relaxed, tired	1	satisfied

list the *cues* that caused you to eat inappropriately (your *behavioral responses*) and their *consequences*. Remember that the settings and consequences that cause you to overeat might be quite different from those that influence someone else.

What are the eating habits that work against you? Do you always have a can of carbonated beverage in hand when you study? Do you eat whenever you are upset? Do you commonly delay doing tasks you don't like by fortifying yourself with a "little snack" first?

A common cue that causes people to eat when they are not hungry is the mere presence of food. "I wasn't hungry; I don't know why I ate that dessert (or extra roll, or huge helping of potato salad)," a person might moan, "except that it was there."

If that is a problem for you—and in this paragraph we are briefly jumping ahead and giving some suggestions for changes—make sure that food will not persistently "be there" (cue control). When shopping, always use a list, and only take a limited amount of money so you do not overstock your cupboards or refrigerator. Once the food is in the house, don't leave it where it is visible. During a meal, don't put serving dishes on the table; leave them somewhere else in the kitchen. If you're in a restaurant and there is still food on your plate after your hunger is satisfied, ask the waiter to remove the plate, or push your chair back from the table a bit so that you can still talk with people easily but find it awkward to eat any more.

Sometimes, particular activities and settings induce people to eat: for example, reading in bed, studying in the living room, watching TV in the student union. What's needed here is to resolve to eat only in selected places: at the kitchen table in your apartment, in the union cafeteria, in restaurants.

For some people, emotional states such as stress, boredom, insecurity, or depression are strong cues for eating. If eating makes you feel less miserable, you will eat again when you experience these feelings (negative reinforcement). If that is true for you, and it has made you overweight, you need other ways to get rid of your bad feelings. If you eat to reduce anxiety, then you might try relaxation training or aerobic exercise as stress-reducing replacements for eating (counterconditioning). Similarly, if boredom or depression are frequent cues for eating, then have a range of interesting and rewarding activities available that can reduce these feelings so that you won't feel you have to resort to eating for this purpose.

For many people, the problem lies in the behavior itself: their rate of eating is too fast. Before they have had enough time to sense that they have had enough, they may have already overeaten. For many people who eat fast, chewing is the cue for swallowing, and swallowing is the cue for taking another mouthful of food; as soon as one mouthful is swallowed, more food goes into the mouth.

Counterconditioning can help here. What's needed is for chewing to become the cue for savoring the taste and texture of food, and for swallowing to become the cue for a time delay that allows a person to sense whether he or she is still hungry or not. Eating more slowly, then, allows a person to attain physiological and psychological satiety (satisfaction) with less food. Fast, unsatisfying overeating is thought to be so common that some eating behavior therapists now focus primarily on helping people slow down their rate of eating, appreciate each bite of food maximally, and become more sensitive to hunger and satiety signals.

Whatever you decide to do to change your eating habits, though, make sure that your new diet provides the nutrients you need. You can check this quickly by being sure it includes at least the minimum recommendations of the Basic Food Guide.

Exercise habits   As far as exercise is concerned, the major question for most people is, "Do you get enough?"

Remember that the general guideline for the minimal amount of exercise needed to maintain cardiovascular fitness is not all that much: you can do it with as little as 15 minutes of vigorous aerobic activity three or four times per week, at an intensity that keeps your heart rate within your training range. Chapter 5 described how to design a program to achieve this for yourself.

But even though this amount of activity helps maintain aerobic capacity, it will probably not help significantly with weight loss. To lose weight, you need to increase your daily energy expenditure by 10 percent (or 20 percent if you exercise every other day).

To determine how many kcalories this represents, refer back to the bottom line of Self-check 4.3 for your total daily energy expenditure. (If Self-check 4.3 does not reflect your current exercise habits, revise it before going further.) Then determine what 10 percent (or 20 percent) of your daily energy expenditure is to see how much you need to increase your energy output.

You can expend this extra amount in any way you choose. One obvious way is to put on your sweatsuit, shorts, or swimsuit more often and add more workouts to your weekly schedule. On the other hand, it may be more time efficient to incorporate the additional activity into your existing routines. You could, for example, just add 15 extra minutes to your current exercise sessions. Or you might modify your daily activities slightly in ways that expend more kcalories: walk up stairs instead of taking elevators, walk a couple of extra blocks to class by getting off the bus a stop earlier, or even bike or walk rather than take the bus. Such changes, practiced consistently, can contribute significantly to weight loss and subsequent weight control.

Implementing your plan

As you begin on your program, remember that you will need reinforcement, and lots of it. Give it liberally to yourself, with such techniques as positive self-talk, and activities or objects that are "treats" for success in practicing the new behaviors. Ask somebody close to you to do the same for you—to react neutrally to your failures, and show genuine praise and support for your successes. Compliments are always nice . . . even if people have been primed to give them.

In addition, you'll probably get some spontaneous compliments from other people as they start to notice the results of your new behaviors; enjoy them! You might stumble onto some pleasant surprises by yourself, like how much easier it is to move between the rows of chairs in the classroom since you dropped a few pounds.

Monitoring your progress

How are you doing? Monitor your progress periodically. Weekly is probably often enough, since changes in body fat take time to occur. Checking more often may make progress seem too slow, but people vary in their reaction to that.

Other Ways to Lose Weight

You might wonder why we haven't endorsed at least some of the hundreds of methods for losing weight that have been promoted in the last few years. What about all the diet books that have been published? The pills that are supposed to promote weight loss? The exercise equipment that promises spot weight reduction? The special suits, wraps, earrings, glasses, and creams that claim to take off pounds?

We will not deal with them one-by-one; sheer volume makes that impossible. Furthermore, diets and weight loss products come and go— mainly because they don't do the job in the long run, sometimes because they cause harm to people, and occasionally because they're illegal.

In order to gain our endorsement, a program for weight loss and long-term weight maintenance would have to be:

- EFFECTIVE: it needs to include both diet and exercise components that result in 1 to 2 pounds of fat loss per week.
- SAFE: it needs to be nutritionally adequate while creating an energy deficit of 500 to 1000 kcalories per day until desirable weight has been achieved.
- FLEXIBLE: it must allow for some individualization of the program in regard to timing of exercise and meals and choice of foods.
- FEASIBLE: it must consist of affordable and readily available foods.
- MAINTAINABLE: it must fit well enough with other aspects of a person's lifestyle to be a suitable framework for permanently healthy eating and exercise habits.

Although an occasional program that becomes popular meets these criteria, probably 98 percent of them do not. After all, most people want to lose weight quickly and effortlessly, which is not consistent with doing it safely and in a way that will last.

The following paragraphs will explain more specifically why we are not enthusiastic about the approaches used in most of the weight-control programs that are currently being sold.

Weight-loss drugs

Many different drugs, both over-the-counter and prescription types, are being sold as aids to decrease food intake, increase energy output, or produce fluid loss. Unfortunately, each drug has one or more negative effects, such as nervousness, body mineral imbalance, or serious metabolic disturbances.

In addition, long-term results using drug therapy for weight loss are generally poor. Although there is usually some weight loss while the drug is being taken, when its use is discontinued, weight is regained, and often goes above the original level.

Weight-control programs led by nonprofessionals

Groups such as TOPS and Overeaters Anonymous employ various weight-reduction procedures but share the feature of group support. Our major reservation about such approaches is that they are often conducted by people who, although they may be successful at losing weight, do not have a nutrition background. Therefore, even though the leaders often are skilled at motivating people and helping them reduce their energy intake, they often are not knowledgeable about nutrition in general. As a result, the nutritional quality of the diets they advocate is sometimes poor. Another problem with such programs is that the group leaders may not be knowledgeable in behavior modification.

Exercise equipment and weight-loss gadgets

Some exercise equipment—such as stationary bikes, treadmills, and rowing machines—can provide as good an aerobic workout as a real bicycle or rowboat, as we discussed in Chapter 6. They can also be helpful as part of a weight-loss or weight-maintenance program. However, some other gadgets are not useful. For example, neither electrical muscle stimulators nor vibrating machines can bring about fat loss because the amount of energy expended in their use is so small that they are ineffective for fat reduction.

Advertisements for these products sometimes claim that they are effective for *spot* reduction, but this is not true either: it is not possible to reduce fat in a particular area of the body by exercising the muscles in that region. Studies have been done in which one side of the body was exercised more than the other, and results did not show any greater loss in body fat on the exercised side. In tennis players, for example, although the dominant arm showed greater muscular development, fat thickness was not different in the two arms (Montoye et al., 1980).

Severe weight-loss diets

Weight-loss diets, in order to sell well, promise dramatic results. To achieve such results, the diets are often extremely low in kcalories—sometimes less than 1000 kcalories per day. Note, though, that it is virtually impossible to meet a person's nutritional needs on such diets: weight-reduction diets should never fall below 1200 kcalories per day.

At worst, very low kcalorie diets can kill people. For example, during the 1970s, over 60 people who were on liquid protein diets died. Fortunately, death is not the usual outcome; less severe (but still very serious) consequences are more likely, such as nutritional deficiencies, impaired immune function, and decreased stamina, strength, and sense of well-being.

Another problem is that severe dietary restrictions seem to put people at risk of subsequent bingeing (Ruderman, 1986). Since it is easily possible to consume in one binge the kcalories "saved" in several prior days of extreme dieting, the weight loss is cancelled out. Various studies have shown that 75 to 95 percent of people who initially lose weight by dieting regain the weight.

When dieters binge, they are likely to experience guilt and shame; this may cause them to eat even more as self-punishment, or to return to their diets with even greater resolve—and then experience another failure. This "rhythm method of girth control" is both physically and psychologically damaging. It causes people to think of themselves as failures for not being able to stick to a diet. Actually, they have been driven off the diet by very powerful physiological and psychological forces. When a person's body senses that it is being seriously deprived of energy, it will recognize the situation as potentially life-threatening, and cause the individual to eat more in order to survive.

Another consequence of very low kcalorie diets is that energy is conserved; energy metabolism becomes more efficient, so that fewer kcalories are needed. That means that weight loss slows down. In addition, when the person starts eating more kcalories again, rapid weight regain is likely. People who used to keep their weight stable on 1800 kcalories per day may now have to limit intake to 1500 kcalories to avoid weight gain. This is a serious price to pay for overzealous dieting.

The point is that with dieting that is too restricted, the outcomes are all negative: there is no sustained weight loss, nutritional status may deteriorate, there is considerable psychological discomfort, and subsequent weight regain is very likely.

Diets that attempt to cut out a major food component are also risky. Low-carbohydrate diets are examples of this: they make unusual metabolic demands on the body, which causes fluid loss and possible dehydration. In some cases, such diets may lead to menstrual disorders, kidney failure, or other problems. Since much of the weight lost is simply water, people are likely to regain weight quickly when they discontinue these diets.

Despite the strong forces that usually cause people to go off severely restricted diets, some people manage to stay on them long enough to lose substantial amounts of weight. This may be destructive in yet another way: it may lead to an eating disorder, as the next section describes.

Eating Disorders

Anorexia nervosa: An eating disorder in which the person starves herself or himself.

Occasionally, maintaining a program that unduly restricts kcalories and demands excessive exercise leads to an eating disorder commonly called **anorexia nervosa**. This condition, most often seen in adolescent girls, can result in the loss of 25 percent or more of body weight. Among the factors that predispose a person to such self-starving behaviors are social pressures to be thin, problems in family interaction, and a strong need for control; but since it is known that dieting precedes many cases of anorexia nervosa, the practice of dieting—especially severe dieting in female teens—carries risk.

Another type of eating disorder that may occur in chronic dieters (again, usually female) is bingeing, eating amounts of food that are many times more than they need, such as 10,000 kcalories at one time. Bingers eat alone, and usually stop only when they are so uncomfortable that they cannot continue, or they fall asleep, or somebody interrupts them. Many chronic bingers purge their gastrointestinal tracts after eating by vomiting or taking enemas or laxatives; they are said to have **bulimia**. Since there is much overlap between these conditions and a wide variety of terms are used to describe them, distinctions between them are often blurred.

Bulimia: An eating disorder characterized by bingeing and purging.

All of these conditions are primarily psychological problems that call for both nutritional and psychological therapy.

It is in a person's best interest to get prompt treatment for an eating disorder if it is suspected that he or she has one. Due to the affected person's preoccupation with eating and not eating, an eating disorder seriously disrupts a person's life and may even result in death. Unfortunately, the person may deny that a problem exists, especially in the case of anorexia nervosa, which means that it is up to others who are close to the individual to see that he or she gets help.

A few simple questions people can ask themselves to help them decide whether they might benefit from evaluation for an eating disorder are shown in Self-check 11.2.

Finally, the sooner a person with an eating disorder begins treatment, the better the chances of dealing with the problem effectively.

Prevention Is Best

We have said a lot about weight control. The following paragraphs summarize the key ideas.

Self-check 11.2   Screening yourself for an eating disorder

Although you cannot diagnose eating disorders in yourself or others by answering these questions, the answers can help you decide if professional evaluation might be a good idea:

- Do you usually eat more than 1000 kcalories above or below your daily energy needs?
- Does it take you more than one-half hour to eat a meal or snack when you are eating alone and are not involved in another activity at the same time?
- Do you have an unusually low body weight?
- For women, has menstruation stopped for reasons other than the onset of menopause?
- Does eating or the anticipation of eating create strong negative feelings in you, such as dread or disgust?
- Do you fear that once you start to eat foods that you enjoy, you will not be able to stop eating?

An answer of "yes" to any of these questions indicates abnormal eating. One such answer does not mean that a person has an eating disorder, but more than one would make the matter worth checking.

If it seems warranted, seek out a health care professional who is experienced in working with people who have eating disorders. If you don't know of any, talk with your major health care provider, or write to the following organizations which publish lists of the names and addresses of such specialists:

- National Anorexia Aid Society
  530 South Cleveland Avenue
  Suite F
  Westervelt, OH 43081
- Anorexia Nervosa/Bulimia Association, Inc.
  133 Cedar Lane
  Teaneck, NJ 07666

Remember, these questions are not diagnostic criteria for eating disorders; they are simply designed to identify some characteristics of abnormal eating.

Body weight has a major impact on health. Although no single standard is the absolute authority as to what a person should weigh, guidance can be taken from height/weight tables, skinfold measurements, and an understanding of one's set-point.

If you weigh more than you should, the best way to lose weight is to moderately decrease your kcaloric intake and increase your exercise to create an energy deficit that results in 1 to 2 pounds of fat loss per week. Behavior modification can help in making these changes.

Very low kcalorie diets are not likely to result in lasting weight loss, and may even make it more difficult to prevent weight gain, or may lead to eating disorders. Weight-loss drugs and gadgets also have poor track records.

The inevitable conclusion is that prevention is better than treatment. In general, people who eat primarily in response to their hunger, stop when they are satisfied, and get at least a moderate amount of exercise will achieve and maintain the body weight that is right for them.

Cardiovascular Disease: Reducing Your Risk

12

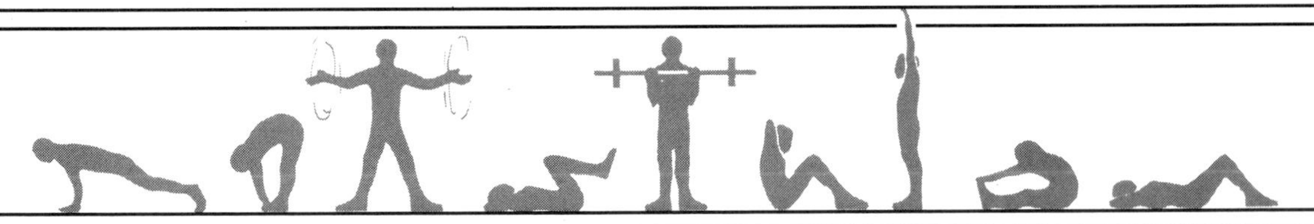

Outline

"Let's get to the heart of the matter." "You gotta have heart." "I don't have the heart to do that."

We often use the word *heart* to refer to something other than the organ that pumps blood through the circulatory system. We use it to mean the central or most vital part of something; courage; compassion; a generous disposition; and as the symbol for love. Such references suggest that even before people had an accurate understanding of the function of the heart, they knew that it was vitally important to their existence.

Cardiovascular (CV) disease: Inclusive term for any of the many diseases that can negatively affect the health of the heart and/or blood vessels.

Here, we will acknowledge the importance of the organ we call the heart by devoting a whole chapter to the role of the heart and the blood vessels and to their health.

When there are problems with this system, we say that a person has **cardiovascular (CV) disease**. Of course, there are many different types of cardiovascular diseases—from inborn structural defects, to disease caused by infection, to conditions that lead to heart attack and stroke. Since heart attacks and strokes are the most prevalent problems, and since the likelihood of their occurrence may be affected by lifestyle, we will confine our discussion to them and to their underlying causes.

The amount of scientific literature on CV disease is vast. Research has been prompted by the fact that almost half of the deaths in the developed countries result from this disease. Many such deaths occur in middle-aged men in their 40's and 50's. Although everybody who experiences a heart attack or stroke does not die immediately from that cause, a person's lifestyle can be considerably restricted as a result of CV disease. This, too, motivates us to learn about the causes, prevention, and treatment of CV disease.

But despite the fact that there has been much research in this area, it still is not completely understood. That is because the types of studies that could tell us definitively what causes it are both unethical and impractical to do. Part of the problem is that CV disease develops over many years. To carry out a definitive study regarding the effect of exercise on the development of heart disease, for example, it would be necessary to completely control the entire lives of matched groups of people who had different physical activity schedules, but whose lives were otherwise kept identical in regard to all other risk factors.

It couldn't be done.

As the next-best approach, two major U.S. studies conducted in Framingham, Massachusetts, and in Tecumseh, Michigan, have been tracking the lifestyles and health status of their residents for decades. These studies and thousands of other investigations in various parts of the world have generated a massive amount of data on CV disease. Animal studies and clinical trials add to this body of knowledge.

Therefore, even though certainty eludes us on many points, much information is already available to help us deal with prevention and treatment of this multifactorial disease. For example, it is recognized that certain habits of living are associated with a greater likelihood of developing CV disease. There is growing evidence (although not unanimous agreement!) that by changing these behaviors, we can significantly reduce the risk of developing this disease. We also know that the sooner a person starts to do something about risk factors, the more likely is the benefit: CV disease begins in many people in the developed countries during childhood and the teenage years.

With the realization that the beginnings of CV disease are already present in most of us, let's look at what it is and what we can do about it, within the limits of our present understanding.

Approximately 40 different risk factors have been identified as being statistically associated with CV disease. Here we will deal with those that have the strongest statistical relationship.

Keep in mind that the existence of a statistical relationship does not prove that the factor *causes* CV disease, but it is *possible* that it does—either directly or in a secondary way.

Analyzing Risk Factors

Uncontrollable factors

First let's recognize that there are some risk factors which cannot be altered, and then quickly move on to those we can do something about.

Heredity plays a role. If there is a high incidence of cardiovascular disease in your family, your likelihood of developing it is greater. *Being male* also increases risk, as does *getting older*.

Race also has an influence; blacks exhibit more CV disease, especially high blood pressure and strokes, than people of other races.

The big three controllable factors

The data on CV disease indicate there are several major risk factors. Fortunately, these are factors which can be altered.

Three of these risk factors stand out as being the most strongly related to the development of heart disease. They are hypertension (high blood pressure), high total blood cholesterol, and smoking.

Hypertension   Blood pressure is the strongest predictor of CV disease risk. In middle-aged adults, for example, blood pressure of 160/90 mmHg is generally regarded as borderline hypertension; anything over that is increasingly dangerous. In younger people, blood pressures considerably lower may be viewed as borderline. Many health care providers believe the diastolic pressure (the lower number) is more significant, since the cardiovascular system maintains this pressure continuously.

Hypertension has been dubbed "the silent killer" because people can have it without knowing it, and it can stress the body to the point of heart attack, stroke, or kidney disease. Since approximately 17 percent of the American public develops hypertension but only a fraction know they have it, recently a public health effort was begun to identify those people so that they can be treated.

Only people who have an inborn predisposition to it will develop high blood pressure, but since there is no way to test for that trait as yet, it is worthwhile for everybody to make use of known preventive measures.

High total blood cholesterol   Another major risk factor for CV disease is high levels of cholesterol in the blood. Some background information is in order here.

Lipoproteins: Combinations of lipids (fats) and proteins; lipoproteins are soluble and are transported in the blood stream.

High-density lipoproteins (HDL): Lipoproteins whose cholesterol does not contribute to the development of CV disease; thought to have a protective effect.

Low-density lipoproteins (LDL): Lipoproteins whose cholesterol may increase the risk of CV disease.

Cholesterol is a type of fat that serves several important functions in the body. It is transported via the bloodstream in compounds called **lipoproteins**.

There are four main types of lipoproteins—high-density, low-density, very-low-density, and chylomicrons. Blood levels of two of them in particular—**high-density lipoproteins (HDL)** and **low-density lipoproteins (LDL)**—influence CV health: having relatively high levels of LDL makes it more likely that a person will develop CV disease, but relatively high levels of HDL have a protective effect.

Typically, LDL predominates: that is, people have several times more LDL than HDL in their blood. Therefore a blood test that measures total cholesterol is largely a measure of LDL concentration. LDL levels are much more variable than HDL levels.

Table 12.1 identifies the levels of total cholesterol corresponding to moderate or to high levels of risk, according to the report of a concensus committee that was convened by the National Institutes of Health (NIH) in 1985. The committee recommended that adult Americans under the age of 30 should try to maintain blood cholesterol levels of approximately 180 milligrams per deciliter (mg/dl; one deciliter is one-tenth of a liter), while those over 30 should maintain no more than 200 mg/dl. Approximately half of the adult American public has levels above 200 mg/dl, which puts them at moderate to high risk.

If a person has a total cholesterol level that indicates risk, a blood test that separately measures the levels of LDL and HDL is usually done. Occasionally it is found that a higher-than-usual HDL level is partly responsible for the high total cholesterol. In such cases, risk is less than if LDL levels are higher than usual.

Smoking   People who smoke cigarettes incur twice the risk of getting CV disease as nonsmokers. Those who start smoking prior to the age of 20 are at greatest risk.

At least 50 million Americans smoke cigarettes regularly, but they are not the only ones whose CV health is affected by their habit; smoke from their cigarettes has a bad effect on the health of nonsmokers as well.

We will not deal extensively with the risks of smoking here; suffice it to say that quitting smoking greatly reduces a person's risk of CV

Table 12.1   Levels of total blood cholesterol for moderate or high risk of CV disease

Age	Blood cholesterol level (mg/dl)	
	Moderate risk	High risk
20–29	200–220	>220
30–39	220–240	>240
40 and over	240–260	>260

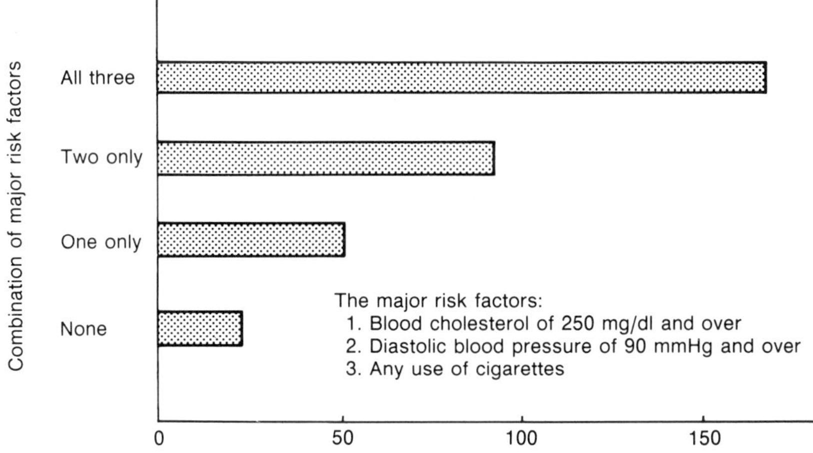

Figure 12.1   How much risk is there in a risk factor? The data from many studies were combined in order to determine the effect on white American males of having one, two, or all three of the major risk factors for heart disease. Each additional risk factor almost doubled the risk of having a heart attack.

disease, as well as many other health problems. (Chapter 2 contains suggestions on how to use behavior modification to quit.)

Figure 12.1 shows the combined results of several studies regarding the effects of these three major factors on the incidence of first heart attacks in white American males.

Several important points stand out:

1. The more of these risk factors the men had, the more likely they were to have a heart attack.
2. If they had none of these three risk factors, only 20 out of 1000 had heart attacks.
3. Even if they had all three of these risk factors, many of the men did not have heart attacks during the period of the study.

Therefore, even though these are the most influential factors, their presence neither guarantees CV disease nor explains all occurrences of it.

Other factors

Other factors that are statistically associated with risk of CV disease are obesity, a high-fat diet, diabetes mellitus, physical inactivity, and the Type A behavior pattern.

A widely accepted theory about how cardiovascular disease begins is that a minor injury to an inside wall of an artery—such as could be

Understanding CV Disease

Atherosclerosis: The progressive accumulation of plaque in arteries.

Coronary heart disease (CHD): Atherosclerosis in the blood vessels that serve the heart.

Stroke or cerebrovascular accident (CVA): Result of interruption of blood flow to the brain.

caused by high blood pressure—creates a roughened region where various materials from the blood can attach and stick. Among the materials that accumulate there are certain blood constituents including cholesterol; the blood vessel then produces new cells in an attempt to smooth over the area. This newly formed material, which is called *plaque*, progressively narrows the lumen, or opening of the blood vessel, and causes the artery to lose its flexibility in that area (Figure 12.2). This condition is called **atherosclerosis**.

Two areas of the body in which the effects of atherosclerosis are most obvious are the brain and the heart. Atherosclerosis in the blood vessels of the heart is called **coronary heart disease (CHD)**.

If the blood vessels that nourish a region of the body have been narrowed considerably, they will not be able to deliver as much oxygen to those areas, and pain may result. This is the case when CHD causes *angina pectoris*, which is experienced as chest pain, but may also involve the left arm and neck, shoulder, or face. When the arteries to the legs are narrowed, leg pain called *intermittent claudication* may result even from a normal amount of walking.

A more critical concern is that the plaque, a blood clot, or a muscular spasm will completely close the narrowed lumen, denying oxygen and nutrients to the cells beyond it; if circulation is not restored within a couple of hours, those cells will die. Another possibility is that the less-flexible blood vessel will not be able to withstand the blood pressure within it, and it will rupture; this also results in cell death.

If such an event occurs in the brain, it is called a **stroke or cerebrovascular accident (CVA)**. Typical symptoms may include loss of consciousness, inability to move voluntarily, and slurred speech.

If it occurs in the blood vessels that serve the heart muscle, the result is called a **heart attack, a myocardial infarction** (myo, muscle; cardial,

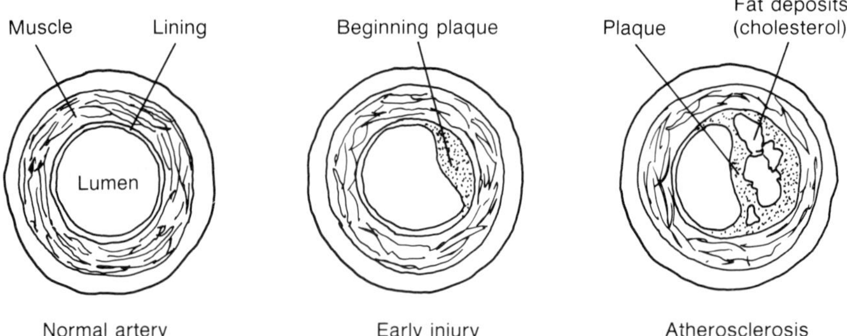

Figure 12.2 Caution: atherosclerosis in process. This disease is thought to begin with a slight roughening of the wall of an artery. Next, materials from the blood begin to collect at the site, progressively narrowing the lumen (the opening of the blood vessel). This process takes place over many years, probably beginning in childhood in the developed countries. The figure shows a cross-section of an artery.

heart; infarction, blockage), or a **coronary occlusion**. Typical symptoms are pain in the chest, stomach, shoulder, and/or back; irregular pulse; and sweating or dizziness.

Although both heart attacks and strokes can result in death, they are not always fatal; it depends on how extensive the damage is, how promptly the person receives care, and what the quality of the care is. It is possible for a person to have such a minor heart attack or stroke that he or she might pass it off as indigestion or dizziness. However, anybody who suspects that a heart attack or stroke is in progress should seek emergency medical treatment immediately.

But let's move beyond this discussion of what happens when a person has CV disease, and use it as a background for learning what can be done to help avoid or delay it.

Heart attack or myocardial infarction or coronary occlusion: Result of interruption of blood flow to the heart.

Exercise Reduces Risk

Several different types of information contribute to what we know about exercise and CV disease.

Epidemiologic studies of exercise

Research on the relationship between heart disease and occupational activity began in 1939, when the histories of approximately 5000 men who lived in Philadelphia and died of heart attacks were studied. The research showed that men who had held sedentary jobs were more likely to die from CHD than would be expected on the basis of their age and sex.

Many more **epidemiologic studies** (studies that involve carefully observing large groups of people) have been done since that time, and almost all of them have shown that men in sedentary occupations tend to die earlier from heart disease than do men in more active lines of work (Kannel et al., 1985; LaPorte et al., 1984).

Epidemiologic study: Observational study of large groups or populations.

However, in and of themselves, such studies are not proof that activity is responsible for the decreased incidence in CHD. It is possible that people who are less prone to heart disease are more likely to select occupations and activities which involve more physical activity. Also, the lack of uniformity in measurement of physical activity among studies makes research results difficult to compare and interpret (LaPorte et al., 1984).

Exercise effects on animals

Laboratory studies using animals demonstrate the beneficial effects of exercise. In one experiment, monkeys who exercised developed less severe cases of atherosclerosis than those who did not exercise, even though they were given diets that promote the disease. Many animal studies show that exercised animals have lower levels of blood cholesterol than sedentary controls. Exercise also appeared to lower blood pressures and delay onset of hypertension in rats.

Of course, these studies describe the effects of exercise on particular animals; the human body cannot be assumed to react in an identical way, although it is possible that it does.

Exercise effects on humans

Exercise is known to have a beneficial effect on blood pressure. When active people are compared with sedentary ones, those who are more active have lower resting blood pressures. Furthermore, when sedentary persons embark on a program of regular exercise, their resting blood pressure generally decreases. These effects are not very large, but even a small decrease in blood pressure reduces the likelihood of a heart attack.

Also, people who get more exercise are leaner, and leaner people tend to have lower total blood cholesterol levels, which puts them at lower risk of CV disease. Exercise decreases low-density lipoproteins in the blood and increases high-density lipoproteins—both being changes that reduce risk.

Problems of exercise

Periodically a newspaper reports that a renowned person has died from a heart attack while exercising. Some people use such isolated incidents to argue that exercise is very risky. If we accept that line of reasoning, since many people die in their sleep, we would also need to believe that sleeping is dangerous.

But let's deal with this issue directly in order to understand the relative hazards of exercise.

Several studies have shown that sudden coronary deaths *are* more likely during or immediately after strenuous physical exertion (Kannel et al., 1985). However, it is important to distinguish between people who are habitually physically active and those who are not. According to one study (Siscovick et al., 1984), compared to sedentary men, habitually active men have only 40 percent as much risk of cardiac arrest both during vigorous physical activity and at all other times; but men with low levels of physical activity had a risk of cardiac arrest during vigorous activity which was 56 times higher than their risk at other times! This says that vigorous exercise for the person who is "out-of-shape" is risky.

The conclusion is clear: adults who have been inactive should begin to exercise in a *well-supervised fitness program that involves a very gradual increase in physical activity*, as described in Chapter 5. Once a person has become more fit, his or her CV system will be better able to withstand more vigorous activity.

Exercise recommendations for reducing risk

There is widespread belief among researchers that exercise reduces the risk of CV disease, especially coronary heart disease or CHD. From there on, it is difficult to find agreement among the experts on just what type or how much exercise is helpful. Nonetheless, people need guidance in planning their exercise programs.

In 1978 the American College of Sports Medicine (an organization of physical educators, physicians, and physiologists primarily) published a position paper on how adults can maintain overall fitness, including CV health. The paper's recommendations were that all healthy individuals should get 15 to 60 minutes of aerobic activity (depending on intensity) three to five times per week. These recommendations still stand.

A study published in 1984 (Paffenbarger et al.) put activity recommendations in different terms—that of kcalories expended per week. This study of almost 17,000 Harvard alumni recorded causes of death over a 16-year period. A wealth of information collected on these men enabled investigators to draw statistical relationships between death from CV disease and factors such as level of athletic activity in college, physical activity level as alumni, smoking status, weight/height ratio, blood pressure status, and family CV health history.

Regarding exercise, it was found that alumni who expended 2000 kcalories or more per week in sports, walking, and stair-climbing were less likely to develop CV disease than those who expended fewer exercise kcalories. Alumni who expended less than 500 kcalories per week in these activities were at greatest risk, and those who expended intermediate amounts were at intermediate risk.

Previous studies have shown that being a college athlete did not prevent subsequent CV disease, unless the person continued to be physically active.

Nutrition can affect two of the three risk factors that are most clearly associated with CV disease—high blood cholesterol and hypertension. Various health agencies and professional organizations have issued guidelines to help Americans reduce these risk factors through diet.

Nutrition Lowers Risk

Diet and blood cholesterol

In 1985, an expert committee organized by the National Institutes of Health (NIH) issued diet recommendations for lowering cholesterol levels. In 1986, the American Heart Association (AHA) published a report called *Dietary Guidelines for Healthy American Adults*. Both reports made similar recommendations about how to control blood cholesterol: maintain ideal weight; limit fat in the diet, especially saturated fat; and limit dietary cholesterol.

The paragraphs that follow discuss these major points.

Avoid overweight   It is known that weight gain is frequently accompanied by an increase in blood cholesterol; a later loss of weight usually decreases the blood cholesterol level. Therefore it is a very useful preventive measure to attain and maintain normal body weight.

We list it first, because for the overweight person who has a high blood cholesterol level, it may be the most effective means of reducing blood cholesterol.

Limit fat in the diet It is recommended that people limit fat in their diets to no more than 30 percent of kcalories. This is because epidemiologic data show that populations with high fat intakes generally have higher blood cholesterol levels and a higher incidence of heart disease, whereas lower intakes are associated with less risk. Since the average U.S. intake of fat is high (close to 40 percent of kcalories), this recommendation calls for a substantial reduction in fat intake.

Both the NIH group and the AHA recommend that less than one-third of a person's fat intake should be saturated fat, since high levels of saturated fat in the diet cause blood cholesterol to rise. The term **saturated fat** refers to fat molecules that contain as much hydrogen as possible in their structures. Saturated fats are primarily found in animal products, such as the fat on and in meat, and the fat in dairy products. However, two commonly used plant oils—coconut and palm oils—are also highly saturated.

Americans typically consume more than one-third of their fat kcalories from saturated fat, so this recommendation calls for dietary changes.

If no more than one-third of the fat in the diet should be saturated, that means that the other two-thirds should be *unsaturated*. Unsaturated fats have the desirable characteristic of being able to lower blood cholesterol levels.

Unsaturated fats can be categorized into **polyunsaturated fats** (having several places in their structures that could accommodate more hydrogen) or **monounsaturated fats**. Polyunsaturates are abundant in plant oils such as corn oil, soybean oil, and safflower oil.

Many studies point to the cholesterol-lowering ability of polyunsaturates, but *a few* studies done on animals given *very* high levels of the polyunsaturates found in plants yielded a disturbing finding—a higher incidence of cancer. For this reason, the NIH recommendations suggest that polyunsaturates in the diet be limited to 10 percent of kcalories, a level thought to confer CV benefit without increasing cancer risk.

Fish oils are also highly polyunsaturated, but their structures include unique fatty acids (not found in plant oils) that reduce CV disease risk. The predominant one is called EPA (eicosapentaenoic acid), and it occurs most notably in fish that live in deep, cold waters, such as anchovies, herring, mackerel, salmon, lake trout, tuna (both fresh and canned), and whitefish.

Several studies point to substantial CV benefits of eating these fish—or whale or seal, which also contain EPA. Among them was a study

Saturated fats: Fats whose molecular structures contain the largest possible number of atoms of hydrogen; usually such fats are of animal origin.

Polyunsaturated fats: Fats whose molecular structures have room for two or more atoms of additional hydrogen.

Monounsaturated fats: Fats whose molecular structures have room for one atom of additional hydrogen.

documenting that Eskimos, despite a high fat diet, had low levels of blood cholesterol and very little death from heart disease. Another was a 20-year study done in the Netherlands which found that men who consumed at least an ounce of fish per day experienced 50 percent fewer deaths from coronary disease than those who did not eat fish (Kromhout et al., 1985). The authors of this study concluded that the consumption of as little as one or two fish dishes per week may be of preventive value. The fish oil issue is a lively area of current research; more will be known in the future about the preventive effects of this oil. At present, the recommendation is to eat one or two fish meals per week.

What about the monounsaturated fats? They are found primarily in nuts, olives, and avocados. Earlier they were thought to be neutral in their effect on blood cholesterol, but some recent research shows they also can lower blood cholesterol. More research is needed before specific advice about their intake can be given.

Limit dietary cholesterol   Americans typically consume between 500 and 600 mg of cholesterol daily. The NIH group, however, recommends cutting current intakes in half to no more than 250–300 mg. The AHA is even more restrictive: they suggest consuming no more than 100 mg of cholesterol per 1000 kcalories ingested, up to a limit of 300 mg of cholesterol.

Cholesterol is found only in foods of animal origin; the most potent sources are eggs and liver (Table 12.2).

Surprisingly, the cholesterol content of the diet has less effect on blood cholesterol levels than do any of the other factors listed here. That is partly because we obtain only about half of our cholesterol from the food we eat. Food is not our main source of cholesterol: our bodies produce it—usually more than we get from our diet. Nonetheless, some people achieve a modest reduction in blood cholesterol by lowering their intake of dietary cholesterol.

Overall, then, a good-for-your-heart diet consists of lots of *fruits and vegetables; grain products; low-fat dairy products,* such as skim and 1 percent milk, and lower-fat cheeses such as cottage cheese; and *fish, legumes,* and *lean meats and poultry.*

Before ending this section, we should note that not all health-concerned groups suggest that everybody should adopt these dietary modifications. Most notably, the American Medical Association recommends major diet changes only for those with evidence of CV disease or a family history of it.

Diet and high blood pressure

Nutrition-related factors that are useful for helping control high blood pressure (hypertension) are avoiding overweight and excessive intake of sodium.

Let's look at these individually.

Table 12.2 Cholesterol levels in some foods

Food	Amount	Cholesterol (mg) 0 100 200 300 400 500
Fruits and vegetables		
All types	½ c	a
Grain products		
Bread, plain	1 slice	
Cake	1 piece	x[b]
Cereal, pasta, grains	½ c	
Egg noodles	½ c	xx
Milk and milk products		
Milk, whole	1 c	xx
Milk, 2%	1 c	x
Milk, skimmed	1 c	
Cheese, cheddar	1⅓ oz	xx
Ice cream	1½ c	xxxxx
Meats and alternates		
Beef, lean cuts	3 oz	xx
Beef, fatty cuts	3 oz	xxx
Chicken, not fried	3 oz	xx
Fish, not fried	3 oz	xx
Eggs	2 medium	xxxxxxxxxxxxxxxxxxxxxx
Legumes, nuts	½ c	
Liver, calves'	3 oz	xxxxxxxxxxxxxx
Limited extras		
Alcoholic beverages	1 serving	
Butter	1 T	x
Cream cheese	1⅓ oz	xx
Mayonnaise	1 T	
Vegetable oils	1 T	

[a]Where no x is shown, little or no cholesterol is present.
[b]Each x represents 25 mg of cholesterol.

Avoid overweight   Many people, if they gain weight, experience a rise in blood pressure. If they lose that surplus weight, their blood pressure decreases, but it does not always completely decrease back to normal. (This is one reason why it is bad for people to repeatedly gain and lose weight; blood pressure may rise a little higher each time.) Since you don't know whether you are one of the people whose pressure will rise as weight is gained, it is in your best interest not to gain the weight in the first place.

Avoid excessive intake of sodium   Epidemiologic studies show that populations that consume a lot of sodium tend to have higher blood pressures than those that consume less sodium. Further, clinical studies have shown that people with high blood pressure can lower it to some extent by severely restricting their intake of sodium. Finally, sodium restriction improves the effectiveness of drugs designed to help lower blood pressure. For these reasons, researchers believe that limiting sodium intake will help forestall and/or control high blood pressure in susceptible individuals.

The AHA recommends that sodium intake be limited to 1000 mg per 1000 kcalories ingested, and should not exceed 3000 mg per day. Considering that sodium is an essential nutrient, you might wonder whether limiting your intake could put you at risk of becoming sodium-deficient. That's not very likely, since the safe and adequate intake range for sodium is 1100 to 3300 mg per day for an adult, whereas the average intake for Americans is 3900 to 4700 mg.

Although sodium occurs in foods as produced by nature, the great majority of sodium enters the diet from salt used commercially in processing and from salt added at home. (Common table salt is 40 percent sodium by weight.) Table 12.3 shows the sodium content of foods from nature as well as the sodium content of foods after processing. You can reduce your sodium intake by eating less of the foods that are generally high in sodium, such as lunchmeat, canned tuna fish and seafood, canned and dehydrated soups, and cheese. Since there is considerable variation in sodium among these and other products, check

Table 12.3 Sodium content of foods from nature and processed food[a]

Food from nature	Sodium (mg per serving)	Processed food	Sodium (mg per serving)
1 cup milk	122	1 c buttermilk (salted)	257
		1½ oz processed cheese	609
3 oz cooked meat (unsalted)	59	3 oz ham	1114
1/2 c fruits, most vegetables	less than 10	1/2 c frozen peas	92
		1/2 c canned peas	247
		1/2 c sauerkraut	777
		1 dill pickle	928
1/2 c grains	less than 10	1 slice bread	114
		1 pancake	152
		1 c broth (from cube)	1152
		Big Mac	1010
		Dairy Queen Super Dog	1552
		1 teaspoon butter	39
		1 teaspoon salt	1938

[a]These figures do not include salt added by the consumer.

whether the nutrition labels state how much sodium is present in products you are considering. When cooking at home, gradually cut down on the amount of salt called for in recipes, and take the salt shaker off your table.

Even if you do all the right things, though, there is no absolute guarantee that restricting sodium will prevent high blood pressure. Some researchers even suggest that we are looking at the wrong nutrient as the causative agent; they argue that rather than too much sodium, shortages of nutrients such as potassium or calcium may promote hypertension. But unless such evidence becomes much more persuasive, public health education efforts will continue to emphasize the potential benefits of limiting sodium intake (Food and Drug Administration, 1984).

Type A Behavior and CHD

A person's behavior pattern may also influence his or her CV disease risk.

What is Type A behavior?

In the 19th century, a few behaviorally astute physicians noted that certain kinds of people were more likely to have heart attacks. More recently, the people most closely associated with that concept are Meyer Friedman and Ray Rosenman, two cardiologists who have treated many people with heart disease.

In the 1950s, Friedman and Rosenman began to recognize common characteristics in people suffering from heart disease. They noticed, for example, that the people in their waiting room seemed to be quite impatient, as evidenced, in part, by the fact that the upholstery at the front edges of the seats tended to wear out first. The heart patients seemed to be literally "on edge." Such observations led them to hypothesize that a particular behavior pattern, which they named the **Type A Behavior Pattern (TABP)**, was a cause of heart disease.

In a 1974 book entitled *Type A Behavior and Your Heart* they described the person with such a pattern as ". . . aggressively involved in a chronic, incessant struggle to achieve more and more in less and less time, and if required to do so, against the opposing efforts of other things or other persons" (Friedman and Rosenman, 1974, p. 84).

Here is their description (slightly modified) of one of their patients:

> Mr. A. is a 43-year-old building contractor. He arrives 45 minutes early and paces in the waiting room as he anxiously awaits his physician's arrival. When his doctor is late, he becomes irritated and impatient, often displaying frustration and hostility by making statements such as, "I'm busy too. In my business if I'm late I would lose a customer!" His speech is rapid, loud and clipped. He frequently emphasizes certain key words by talking louder or gesturing with his hands. When he talks with the doctor he seems to be superficially involved in the conversation but he

Type A Behavior Pattern (TABP): Pattern of behaviors characterized by time urgency, hostility, and competitiveness; thought to be a risk factor for CHD.

isn't really listening. He seems more intent on asking questions and, in general, controlling the conversation. He is very involved with his work, with his family being of secondary interest.

The Type A behavior pattern has three major characteristics—time urgency, hostility, and competitiveness. A strong positive reinforcer for Type A people is outshining other people in as many areas as possible. In their efforts to outdo others, Type A people may "step on" others and display hostile behaviors. And since Type A people want their rewards as quickly as possible, they are impatient and feel anxious and stressed if their efforts are interrupted. When they do reach their goal, they immediately strive for additional rewards, rather than stopping to enjoy what they've achieved.

Type A behavior as a risk factor

Rosenman and Friedman had put their hypothesis to the test in controlled studies before they wrote their book. One study, the Western Collaborative Group Study (1964), involved over 3000 middle-aged men who were free of CHD symptoms at the beginning of the study. The researchers collected data on the subjects' cholesterol and blood pressure levels, smoking habits, and Type A tendencies.

It was found that men who exhibited Type A behavior were about twice as likely to develop CHD as men who did not. This was true whether or not they smoked, had high blood pressure, or a high level of cholesterol.

Additional studies over the past 20 years have tended to confirm a link between Type A behavior and heart disease in both men and women. Recently, a government panel concluded that the TABP was an independent risk factor for coronary heart disease (The Review Panel on Coronary-Prone Behavior and Coronary Heart Disease, 1981).

Friedman and his co-workers have studied whether reducing Type A behavior also reduces heart attacks (Friedman et al., 1984). This research involved men who were recovering from heart attacks. The experimental group, in addition to receiving the standard medical care and counselling given to such patients, were given help in reducing their Type A tendencies; the control group received only the standard treatment. The men in the experimental group showed a greater decrease in Type A behavior, and were less likely to have another heart attack than those in the control group.

The participants in this study were men with established CHD. Can we assume that reducing Type A behavior in *healthy* people would lower their risk of CHD? Many experts believe that such an approach would be useful; others are less convinced that becoming less impatient, competitive, and hostile would make you less prone to heart disease. In addition, there has been some recent disagreement about whether or not the TABP actually does cause coronary heart disease. Our opinion is that there is sufficient evidence to justify reducing Type A behavior.

Assessing and changing Type A behavior

Researchers and clinicians often use the Jenkins Activity Survey (Jenkins et al., 1979) and the Structured Interview (Rosenman et al., 1964) to determine whether an individual has the TABP.

If you took the Jenkins Activity Survey, you would respond to paper-and-pencil, multiple-choice questions about your behavior. For example: do you eat more rapidly than most people, refuse to wait in line, and get irritated easily? Your score on the test would be compared with the scores of other college students, or some other appropriate comparison group. In the Structured Interview you would answer a standard series of questions designed to elicit Type A behavior. The interviewer would have been trained both to record your answers and also to observe the way you answer the questions for evidence of Type A behavior. For example: do you get impatient if the interviewer hesitates or do you run your words together in responding?

You probably do not have easy access to these tools for assessing the TABP. However, what we've said about them, in addition to our other descriptions of Type A behavior, should give you a feeling for what to look for in yourself and others.

If you believe you are a Type A person and want to reduce this trait, how can you go about it?

First of all, you might consider *cue control* procedures. Try to determine the cues for your Type A behavior and then eliminate them, or at least make them less prominent. Arrange your work area so that there is a minimum of clutter. Try to work on one task at a time and have available only the material you need for that task. But restrict your exposure to work cues to certain hours of the day, reserving other times for calming, relaxing activities: build some "quiet time" into your life. Introduce cues for relaxation and leisure into your living area, such as an easy chair, or travel and recreation posters.

Counterconditioning can also be used. Identify situations that lead to Type A behaviors for you, and then practice new behaviors in these situations. For example, if waiting in line to buy a theater ticket or waiting for a red traffic light to change makes you feel impatient, you can relax by using progressive muscle relaxation (as described in Chapter 7) when you find yourself in those situations.

Finally, you can *examine the events and things which serve as rewards* for you. Some researchers believe that a basic characteristic of the Type A person is that he or she seldom derives satisfaction from achieving a goal, and almost never from the behavior involved in reaching the goal. Rather, for such a person achieving something is a cue for striving for something more. The phrase "joyless striving" has been used to describe such behavior.

If you recognize yourself in this description, you might make a point of stopping after you reach a goal to enjoy what you've achieved, instead of immediately striving for something else. Further, try to find reinforcement in the process rather than its consequence. If you approach jogging by forever trying to go farther and faster, switch your focus to enjoying the feelings and experiences you have while jogging.

In this chapter we have said a great deal about cardiovascular disease and its prevention. Since CV diseases account for approximately half of the deaths in developed countries, it's encouraging that there has been so much to say.

CV disease develops over many decades, influenced by habits of living as well as various uncontrollable factors. People can take action to reduce risk of CV disease by getting enough exercise; eating a diet that is moderate in kcalories, fats, and salt; quitting smoking; and reducing Type A behaviors.

A final word to the wise: early intervention is the best.

Aging Healthfully 13

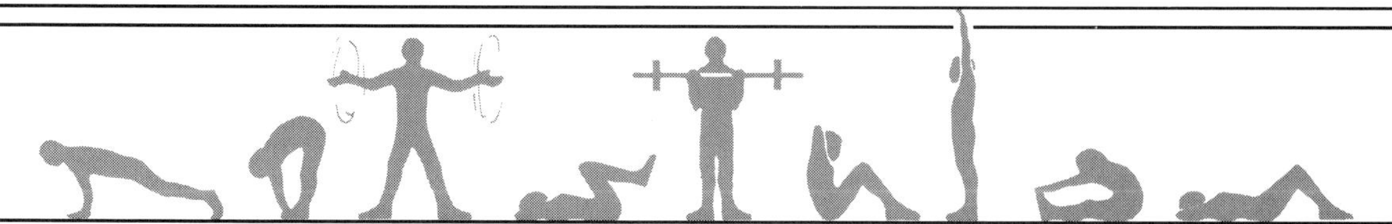

Outline

If you had the choice, how long would you like to live?

Chances are, a large part of your decision would be based on your estimate of how long you might feel and function well enough to enjoy life. Few people want to live a very long life if it means having years of discomfort or disability.

But aging and illness are not synonymous. **Aging** involves a gradual loss of functional capacity that may lessen the vigor and speed with which we do various activities, but it does not necessarily prevent us from doing them. Aging is universal, progressive, irreversible, and time-dependent: we cannot stop it and it happens to everybody.

But much of what we consider aging is not aging at all. Sometimes it is difficult to separate what is true nonpreventable aging from what is a result of changing lifestyles or acquired disability. For example, the decrease in physical fitness which is seen in many older people is, for the most part, the result of a decrease in physical activity.

Aging: The universal, progressive, irreversible, and time-dependent loss of functional capacity that occurs in all living organisms with the passage of time.

237

Another reason we often confuse aging and illness is that statistically speaking, the likelihood of developing an illness increases as we get older. But each person can individually take steps which may prevent or delay illness.

The thrust of this book has been to present, as best we know how, what can be done to avoid or postpone illness, and to achieve and maintain high-quality, healthy living to the extent that exercise, stress reduction, and nutrition practices can help. This chapter continues on that theme.

In this last chapter we will discuss two common problems of bones and joints—osteoporosis and arthritis—that can affect people as they age. We will also concern ourselves with cancer, the number-two killer in the developed countries. And finally, longevity: we will discuss whether the lifestyle changes we advocate make a difference in how long a person lives.

Reducing Your Risk of Osteoporosis

Osteoporosis: A disease involving severe loss in density and/or mass of bone.

Osteoporosis is a disease in which considerable bone mass and/or density is lost. Bones become thin and brittle and are more liable to break than normal bones; the most common fracture sites are the spine, wrist, and hip.

Osteoporosis is a major problem, since it is the cause of over a million fractures annually. Over one billion dollars are spent each year in acute care of hip fractures in the United States (Recker, 1983),and at least 20 percent of people who fracture a hip die less than one year after the injury occurs (Consensus Development Panel, 1984).

Learning how bones are formed will help you understand osteoporosis. Bone is a very dynamic material: throughout a person's life, calcium and other constituents continually move into and out of bone from the bloodstream. During periods of growth, there is a dramatic net gain of materials in bone, so bone mass increases. During early adulthood, the rate of movement in and out is fairly well balanced, and bone mass is relatively stable. Materials moving into bone are involved in a process called *remodeling,* in which old, weakened bone tissue is replaced or strengthened. But starting at around the age of 35, the outgo of bone constituents begins to exceed the amount deposited during remodeling, and bone mass decreases. Figure 13.1 illustrates how much bone can be lost in 14 years.

Figure 13.2 shows typical changes in the thickness of cortical bone (the hard, outer part of long bones) through the life cycle of males and females.

The data indicate that there is considerable difference between men and women in the rate at which they lose cortical bone. However, there is also much variation from one individual to another. It is only when an individual experiences severe losses that the condition is called osteoporosis. As many as 15 to 20 million people in the United States

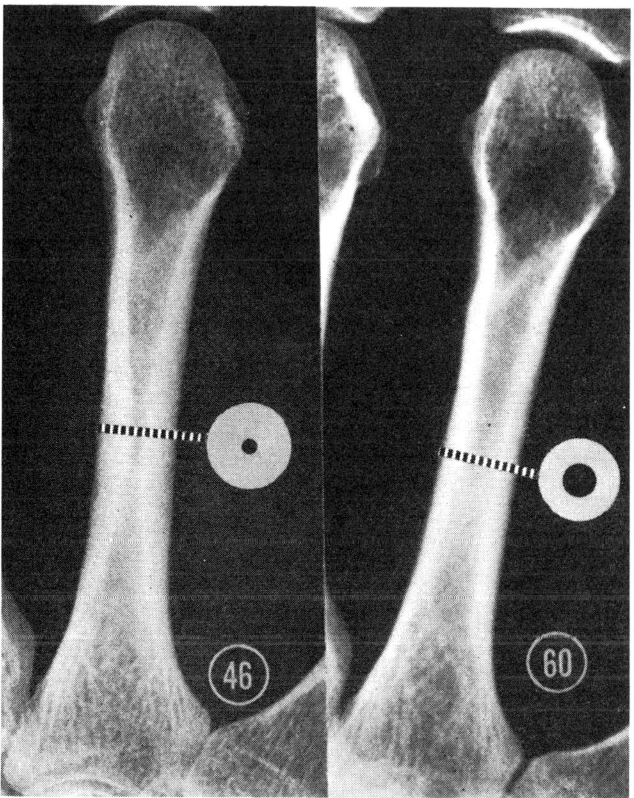

Figure 13.1 X rays showing loss of bone mass. These two x rays of a woman's hand were taken 14 years apart. The x ray on the left shows the original status of the bone; that on the right shows how much thinner the cortical bone (the hard, outer shell) has become in 14 years. The discs diagram cross-sectional views; the numbers (46 and 60) indicate the woman's age when the x rays were taken.

are thought to have osteoporosis, and the incidence is eight times greater in women than men (Consensus Development Panel, 1984).

A number of factors have been linked to risk of osteoporosis. Most of these are related to bone mass and density, the greater a person's bone mass or density, the less likely it is that osteoporosis will occur. Since the skeletal mass of females is about 30 percent less than males at any age, women—especially those with small frames—are at greater risk. Race also plays a role, since whites tend to have less bone mass than blacks.

Gender and race, of course, are factors about which nothing can be done; but there are other factors affecting risk that can be altered. They are discussed below.

Hormonal status

The hormone *estrogen* leads to better calcium retention. The fact that women's bodies produce much less estrogen after menopause helps

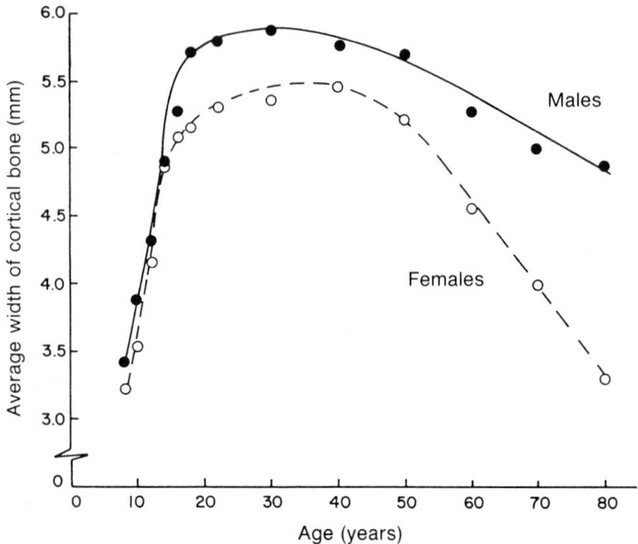

Figure 13.2 Change in bone thickness over time for males and females. In a large study done on residents of the state of Ohio, the cortical bone width of one of the bones in the hand differed with age as shown.

explain the tremendous increase in the rate of bone loss in women after the age of 45 to 50. Women who have stopped menstruating prematurely may also be at greater risk of osteoporosis; much research is going on in this area.

Some health care professionals advocate administration of estrogen supplements when a woman's own estrogen production begins to wane. This method is controversial because of uncertainty about whether it increases the incidence of cancer of the uterus; but this hazard generally can be limited through use of proper doses of estrogen. Women should discuss this with their own health care providers.

Calcium status

Ninety-nine percent of the calcium in the body is located in bone, and a high percentage of bone is composed of calcium. Therefore, it seems logical that inadequate intake, poor absorption, and/or poor utilization of calcium would be among the factors that put a person at greater risk of osteoporosis, but unfortunately it's not that simple. Current research indicates that an inadequate level of dietary calcium *is* a risk factor for osteoporosis, but the relationship is fairly weak; other factors may be more important.

Timing is another issue: although osteoporosis manifests itself during adulthood, waiting until then to take in adequate calcium is unlikely to decrease the risk of osteoporosis. Calcium intake should be on a lifelong basis. A study done on women who had lived their lives in areas of Yugoslavia where the average intake of calcium was approximately 1000 mg per person per day had much greater peak skeletal bone mass and fewer bone fractures than those in areas where average intakes were about 450 mg per day (Matkovic et al., 1979). (However, the diets varied in other ways too, which may have contributed to the difference.) The current hypothesis is that the prime time for reducing risk of osteoporosis by dietary means is during the years of bone growth. In other words, calcium needs to be consumed at high levels during childhood, the teen years, and the 20s and early 30s in order to provide raw materials for developing the greatest possible bone mass within genetic limits.

It is also advantageous to continue adequate calcium intake during the adult years. It has been found that before menopause (and after menopause in women who are receiving estrogen therapy), a dietary calcium intake of 1000 mg per day helps keep bone mass stable. Women after menopause who are not receiving hormone supplements need 1500 mg per day for maintenance (Heany et al., 1978). These levels of intake have been recommended by the Consensus Development Conference on Osteoporosis sponsored by the National Institutes of Health (1984). (Note that such intakes are in excess of the 1980 RDA for adult women for calcium, which is only 800 mg/day.)

Since the average adult American female's intake is only 450 to 550 mg/day, low intake may be a risk factor for many people. There are differences between the sexes in this regard; studies show that women consistently consume less calcium in relation to their needs than men do.

Let's take a look at what a person would need to eat and drink to get 1000 to 1500 mg of calcium. Table 13.1 gives the calcium contents of various types of foods. Note that milk and its products generally furnish the most calcium, with approximately 300 mg per serving. Fish with small, soft, edible bones are the next best if the bones are eaten. After that, there are plants that contain calcium, but the bioavailability of their calcium is generally lessened by certain substances in the food that interfere with calcium absorption and utilization.

Dairy products, then, should be a major source of calcium; a diet that includes three cups of milk or its equivalent can easily provide 1000 mg of calcium; one that includes four servings of milk and its products comes close to 1500 mg of calcium, assuming that other lesser sources are also present in the diet.

What about calcium supplements for people who do not get the recommended amount from their diet? Calcium supplements may help some individuals maintain bone mass, but most studies have not demonstrated this. Furthermore, bones of a person taking supplements are not as resistant to fracture as the bones of a person using dietary sources (Recker and Heany, 1985). Therefore, the tremendous commercial promotion of calcium supplements currently seen in the media is definitely a second-best approach.

Table 13.1 Calcium content of some foods

Food	Amount	Calcium (mg) 0 200 400
Fruits and vegetables		
Apricots, raw or dried	3 whole	[a]
Beans, green snap, cooked	½ c	x[b]
Corn, cooked	½ c	
Peas, cooked	½ c	
Spinach, cooked	½ c	xx
Turnip greens, cooked	½ c	xxx
Grain products		
Bread, whole grain	1 slice	x
Bread, white enriched	1 slice	
Cereal, sweetened puffed wheat	1 oz	
Cereal, shredded wheat	1 oz	
Spaghetti, cooked noodles	½ c	
Milk and milk products		
Milk	1 c	xxxxxx
Yogurt, plain	1 c	xxxxxxxx
Cheese, cheddar	1⅓ oz	xxxxx
Cheese, cottage	2 c	xxxxx
Ice cream	1½ c	xxxxx
Meats and alternates		
Beans, canned with tomato sauce and pork	1 c	xxx
Beef, ground, broiled	3 oz	
Eggs, fried	2	x
Liver, beef, cooked	3 oz	
Peanut butter	¼ c	x
Salmon including bones, canned	3 oz	xxx
Salmon, no bones, cooked	3 oz	
Shrimp	3 oz	xx
Walnuts, English, chopped	½ c	x
Limited extras		
Beer	12 oz	
Butter, margarine	1 t	
Candy, milk chocolate	1 oz	xxx
Carbonated cola beverage	12 oz	
Honey, white sugar	1 T	

[a]Where no x is shown, little or no calcium is present.
[b]Each x represents 50 mg of calcium.

Another few words of caution about calcium supplements are needed. Certain supplements may contain toxic substances: some samples of *bone meal* and *dolomite* have been found to naturally contain lead, arsenic, mercury, or cadmium, so these supplements should not be used. Compounds such as calcium carbonate, calcium gluconate, and calcium lactate do not carry this risk. A final concern is that excessively high intake of calcium may interfere with the absorption of other important minerals, such as iron.

Vitamin D status

An adequate intake of vitamin D is necessary for optimal calcium absorption and metabolism. One study showed that women whose diets are adequate in both calcium and vitamin D have significantly greater bone density than women with inadequate intakes (Sowers et al., 1985). This is why the producers of some calcium supplements include vitamin D in their preparations.

However, vitamin D status is not a problem for most people. For one thing, vitamin D is added to most fluid milk in this country (fortified milk is the best dietary source), and it is present in lesser amounts in eggs and liver. But even if an adult does not consume the recommended amount of vitamin D in the diet, he or she is likely to get as much as is needed from a nondietary source—the sun. Vitamin D is produced in the body when sunlight converts a substance in skin into vitamin D. As little as ten minutes of sun exposure to the face and hands of a light-skinned person (*more* for a dark-skinned person) provides a day's supply. (This rate decreases with age.) Considering the body's ability to convert this substance, there are few people whose vitamin D status is inadequate; such as shut-ins—especially the elderly—who do not consume vitamin D-fortified milk.

Since vitamin D is a nutrient that is toxic when consumed in excess, it makes more sense to be concerned about getting *too much* of this substance than not enough. People who take supplements containing vitamin D should be careful not to exceed the RDA of 400 IU per day from this source. (Long exposure to sun will not result in vitamin D toxicity.)

Exercise status

Bones generally adapt to stresses placed upon them; therefore exercise strengthens bones.

Studies of tennis players demonstrate this well. Since tennis players subject one arm to much more stress than the other, their arm bones can be compared to see the effects of exercise. In a study of professional tennis players in their mid-twenties, every player showed a greater thickness in the upper arm bone on the dominant side by at least 25 percent over the nondominant arm (Jones et al., 1977). Even in older amateur, male tennis players who played fewer hours per week (an average of approximately 8 hours), the upper arm bone was 4 percent wider in the dominant arm and had 13 percent more mineral per centimeter of bone. These differences between arms were much greater than was seen in nontennis players of the same age (Montoye et al., 1980).

The converse is also true: inactivity leads to bone loss. People who are in casts or are immobile for other reasons lose body calcium at the rate of approximately 1 percent every 4 to 6 weeks. In the early Gemini flights, astronauts lost 1 to 2 percent of their bone density per month; therefore, exercise sessions were incorporated into the routines of later space flights.

Certainly, then, a program of moderate exercise is a sound preventive measure. Activities that place gravitational stress on the bones, such as walking, jogging, or tennis, are helpful for maintaining bone mass and density; but swimming, rowing, and bicycling—although excellent activities for improving cardiovascular fitness and controlling body weight—do not have as much impact on bone health.

Levels of exercise as recommended in Chapter 5 are helpful for reducing the risk of osteoporosis.

Other factors

In addition, other factors are statistically associated with osteoporosis. High intakes of alcohol, caffeine, and protein are associated with increased loss of calcium. Cigarette smoking also increases risk of osteoporosis, as does long-term treatment with certain medications such as cortisone (Recker, 1983).

Arthritis Can Be Helped, Not Cured

Arthritis: A group of diseases that affect the joints.

Arthritis, a group of diseases that affect the joints (from arthron, joint in Greek; and -itis, inflammation), is an ancient disease. Archeological digs and Egyptian mummies prove that this problem has been bedeviling mankind for thousands of years.

Even today, an estimated 30 to 40 million Americans suffer from one of the many forms of arthritis; the three most common forms of arthritic diseases are osteoarthritis, rheumatoid arthritis, and gout. Heredity may play a role in whether or not a person develops arthritis.

Although arthritis generally cannot be cured, its pain and crippling effects can often be minimized by prevention, early intervention, and treatment methods.

Osteoarthritis

Osteoarthritis: A form of arthritis in which cartilage in joints becomes roughened and painful from repeated use.

Osteoarthritis, the most common form, is often called the "wear-and-tear" disease. It occurs when overweight, poor posture, or occupational strain repeatedly irritate cartilage, the rubbery material that covers the ends of bones and cushions joints, and lead to its breakdown. It may also be initiated by an acute injury to a joint, such as an injury to the knee from football; in this case it is referred to as *traumatic arthritis.*

Most people over the age of 50 have some degree of osteoarthritis, with women more frequently affected than men. Common symptoms are pain and stiffness, especially in finger joints and those that bear the body's weight—the hips, knees, and spine.

Since this disease most often results from accumulated, lifelong wear on the joints, prevention consists of avoiding overweight, since carrying extra poundage unduly stresses the foot, ankle, knee, and hip joints during many physical activities. It may also help if you choose your sports from among those with less risk of traumatic injury; generally contact sports are riskier than other activities.

If arthritis does occur, there are several helpful measures that can be taken. One such measure is to use medication to control pain. Aspirin is most commonly used, but several other effective medications are also available.

Another important goal is to maintain as much mobility in the affected joints as possible; therefore exercise is a key feature of treatment. Exercise in which body weight is partially supported is especially useful for persons with arthritis in the joints of the lower limbs; examples are swimming, bicycle riding, and rowing. Walking and skiing are also well tolerated, but activities in which there is a lot of sprinting and/or jumping—such as basketball, running, and volleyball—may be painful and cause further damage. A person who needs help planning a program that assures appropriate exercise and rest can get professional help from an orthopedic physician or a physical therapist.

Besides maintaining mobility, other important reasons for a person with osteoarthritis to exercise are to maintain muscle strength, preserve aerobic capacity, and help maintain normal body weight.

As far as nutrition is concerned, our advice will have a familiar ring, because it was also mentioned as a preventive measure: maintain normal body weight to minimize stress on joints. Other than that, there are no effective nutritional treatments for osteoarthritis, according to the National Institute of Arthritis, Metabolism, and Digestive Diseases and the Arthritis Foundation, two agencies that keep careful track of all serious work done on the subject.

The popular press would have you believe otherwise: many useless dietary "cures" are promoted in various books and periodicals, such as fasting; drinking special beverages such as burdock burr tea, celery juice, or distilled water; consuming particular foods, such as alfalfa, blackstrap molasses, pokeberries, watercress, cherries, raw liver, or parsley; avoiding certain foods, such as dairy products, meat, fruit, egg yolk, potatoes, tomatoes, peppers, or eggplant.

Besides these useless dietary treatments, other bogus methods are also marketed, such as copper bracelets, electromagnetic devices, and vibrating chairs. The reason people are so susceptible to useless suggestions is that arthritis is a very unpredictable disease; symptoms come and go for no discernable reason. Because of this, a person with arthritis might credit coincidental, unrelated factors with the relief of the symptoms. The U.S. Food and Drug Administration warns that people should be wary if treatments offer special or secret formulas, promise quick cures, or are based on testimonials without reputable research to support them.

Rheumatoid arthritis

Rheumatoid arthritis (RA): A system-wide form of arthritis in which joints are inflamed and painful.

Rheumatoid arthritis (RA) is the most serious form of arthritis because it is the most crippling. It generally starts between the ages of 20 and 45, affecting three times as many women as men. Although the cause is unknown, many scientists think RA may be initiated by a virus, or involve disruption of the body's immune system.

The current view is that in people with RA the immune system, which normally shields a person against disease, becomes confused and begins to attack and destroy certain body tissues. RA causes inflammation and swelling of the synovial membrane, a layer that lines joints; in addition, chemicals are released which gradually dissolve cartilage and bone ends. However, this disease is not limited to the joints: it can affect many body systems, such as the heart.

The earlier the disease is identified, the more successful the treatment; currently, only one in six people with RA develops a handicapping deformity. Prescription medications are usually needed to help halt the crippling effects, and research is under way to identify and test new drugs. As with osteoarthritis, RA is characterized by a "flare-up and remission" pattern, disappearing and reappearing unpredictably. In about 20 percent of RA cases, at an early stage the disease goes away for good.

For the person with RA, as with osteoarthritis, exercise is important for maintaining general strength, fitness, and flexibility. The dietary treatment consists of a well-balanced diet that helps maintain optimal body weight.

Gout

Gout is the form of arthritis whose treatment has been the most successful. It is the easiest form of the three to understand, diagnose, and treat.

Gout: A form of arthritis characterized by high levels of uric acid in the blood.

Gout is a metabolic disorder that most commonly affects the joints of the feet, especially the big toe. This form of arthritis mainly affects men, who account for nearly all cases.

Gout occurs when an excess of the body chemical uric acid is deposited in the tissues, causing inflammation and severe pain. The feeling has been likened to having ground glass in the joints. Attacks may be prompted by minor injuries, surgery, or excessive exercise, eating, or drinking—or there may be no apparent reason.

At one time a special diet was the major means used to control uric acid levels and treat gout, but now there are prescription drugs that are much more effective than the special diet. Still, some dietary advice is useful: a) maintain ideal body weight (obesity usually is associated with gout); b) avoid fasting and low carbohydrate diets; and c) limit the fat in the diet (Krause and Mahan, 1984). Also, it is better not to drink alcohol on an empty stomach, as this raises uric acid levels.

People who have gout should exercise moderately, keeping in mind that excessive exercise can prompt a gouty attack.

Cancer is the second leading cause of death in the United States. Since nutrition plays a role in an estimated 35 percent of all cancer deaths, it is important to know what dietary practices can help reduce the risk of cancer.

Cancer consists of cells that have uncontrolled growth and spread without normal restraints. Diet is thought to influence cancer risk in three different ways:

1. Food may contain particular substances, called **carcinogens**, that initiate or promote the cancer process.
2. Excessive kcalorie intake may increase risk of cancer.
3. Certain substances in foods (anticarcinogens) may protect against cancer.

Scientists have been studying the relationship between diet and cancer for decades in thousands of experiments. Although research results are not completely consistent, the weight of evidence has allowed scientists to suggest provisional guidelines for reducing the risk of cancer through diet.

In a landmark effort in 1982, the Committee on Diet, Nutrition, and Cancer of the National Academy of Sciences released their summary of the research and offered guidelines for reducing cancer risk. In addition, in 1984, the National Cancer Institute published their recommendations for the public.

The following points summarize the message of the National Cancer Institute's publication *Diet, Nutrition, and Cancer Prevention: A Guide to Food Choices*:

- Eat a varied, well-balanced, moderate diet every day by including foods from each of the basic groups: fruits and vegetables; grain products; meats, poultry, eggs, fish, dry peas, and dry beans; and milk, cheese, and yogurt. This is important for good general health which helps disease resistance.
- Select foods that provide 25 to 35 grams of dietary fiber each day (Table 13.2). Different types of fiber provide different benefits.

Diet May Reduce Cancer Risk

Cancer: A group of diseases characterized by uncontrolled growth of cells that do not respond to normal restraints.

Carcinogen: A cancer-producing substance.

Table 13.2   Fiber content of various foods.

To increase the amount of fiber in your diet, choose several servings of foods each day from the rich and moderately rich fiber sources. Since the dietary fiber content of many foods is still unknown, this is not a comprehensive list. Fiber content for vegetables and fruits that can be eaten with their skins includes fiber content of the skins.

Food	Serving size	Food	Serving size
RICH SOURCES (4 grams or more per serving)			
Breads and cereals		**Legumes** (cooked portions)	
ᵃAll Bran	1/3 cup	Kidney beans	1/2 cup
ᵃBran Buds	1/3 cup	Lima beans	1/2 cup
Bran Chex	2/3 cup	Navy beans	1/2 cup
Corn Bran	2/3 cup	Pinto beans	1/2 cup
Cracklin' Bran	1/3 cup	White beans	1/2 cup
ᵃ100% Bran	1/2 cup		
Raisin Bran	3/4 cup	**Fruits**	
ᵃBran, unsweetened	1/4 cup	Blackberries	1/2 cup
Wheat germ, toasted, plain	1/4 cup	Prunes	3
MODERATELY RICH SOURCES (1 to 3 grams of fiber per serving)			
Bread and cereals		Carrots	1/2 cup
Bran muffins	1 medium	Cauliflower	1/2 cup
Popcorn (air-popped)	1 cup	Corn	1/2 cup
Whole-wheat bread	1 slice	Green peas	1/2 cup
Whole-wheat spaghetti	1 cup	Kale	1/2 cup
40% bran flakes	2/3 cup	Parsnip	1/2 cup
Grapenuts	1/4 cup	Potato	1 medium
Granola-type cereals	1/4 cup	Spinach, cooked	1/2 cup
Cheerio-type cereals	1¼ cup	Spinach, raw	1/2 cup
Most	1/3 cup	Summer squash	1/2 cup
Oatmeal, cooked	3/4 cup	Sweet potato	1/2 medium
Shredded wheat	2/3 cup	Turnip	1/2 cup
Total	1 cup	Bean sprouts (soy)	1/2 cup
Wheat Chex	2/3 cup	Celery	1/2 cup
Wheaties	1 cup	Tomato	1 medium
Legumes (cooked) and nuts		**Fruits**	
Chick peas (garbanzo beans)	1/2 cup	Apple	1 medium
Lentils	1/2 cup	Apricot, fresh	3 medium
Almonds	10 nuts	Apricot, dried	5 halves
Peanuts	10 nuts	Banana	1 medium
		Blueberries	1/2 cup
Vegetables		Cantaloupe	1/4 melon
Artichoke	1 small	Cherries	10
Asparagus	1/2 cup	Dates, dried	3
Beans, green	1/2 cup	Figs, dried	1 medium
Brussels sprouts	1/2 cup	Grapefruit	1/2
Cabbage, red and white	1/2 cup	Orange	1 medium

Continued

Table 13.2   Continued

Food	Serving size	Food	Serving size
MODERATELY RICH SOURCES (1 to 3 grams of fiber per serving) (Continued)			
Fruits (Continued)			
Peach	1 medium	Raisins	1/4 cup
Pear	1 medium	Strawberries	1 cup
Pineapple	1/2 cup		
LOW SOURCES (less than 1 gram of fiber per serving)			
Breads and cereals		**Fruits**	
White bread	1 slice	Grapes	20
Spaghetti, cooked	1 cup	Watermelon	1 cup
Brown rice, cooked	1/2 cup		
White rice, cooked	1/2 cup	**Fruit juices**	
Corn flake-type cereals	1¼ cup	Apple	1/2 cup
		Grapefruit	1/2 cup
Vegetables		Grape	1/2 cup
Lettuce, shredded	1 cup	Orange	1/2 cup
Mushrooms, sliced	1/2 cup	Papaya	1/2 cup
Onions, sliced	1/2 cup		
Pepper, green, sliced	1/2 cup		

[a]Six or more grams of fiber per serving.

- Limit fat to no more than 30 percent of kcalories. This may reduce your risk of cancers of the colon, breast, prostate, or endometrium (lining of the uterus).

- Each week include several servings of cruciferous vegetables (brussels sprouts, cabbage, broccoli, cauliflower, rutabagas, and turnips). They contain an anticarcinogen that seems to protect against cancer of the colon.

- Eat foods that are rich in vitamins A and C (see Figure 10.1). Foods high in vitamin A, such as carrots and spinach, seem to help protect against cancers of the lung, bladder, and larynx; foods high in vitamin C, such as broccoli and oranges, seem to help protect against cancers of the stomach and esophagus. Note that the recommendation is to eat *foods* with vitamins A and C, rather than to take supplements, since other substances in the foods rather than the vitamins themselves may be responsible for the lowered risk.

- Discard moldy foods, because molds produce toxins. One toxin that has been studied extensively, called *aflatoxin*, is a potent liver carcinogen (cancer-producer). Other toxins may have equally dangerous effects.

- Limit intake of alcoholic beverages to two or fewer drinks per day, especially if you smoke. Heavy drinking increases the risk of cancers of the mouth, pharynx, esophagus, liver, and bladder.
- Do less charcoal grilling and frying at high temperatures, since these processes may produce carcinogens in food; it is safer to bake, roast, oven broil, microwave, boil, steam, poach, or stew foods. You can reduce risk from charcoal grilling by wrapping food in foil before cooking or putting it in a pan to reduce its direct contact with the smoke and flames; or raise the grill higher above the coals to cook foods more slowly at a lower temperature.

Effects of a Healthy Lifestyle

We believe that a healthy lifestyle can help you live longer, but it's tough to prove it. This topic provides the ultimate example of the definitive study that is ethically and administratively impossible to perform.

One of the many challenges in studying this issue is that there may be a strong genetic component to the length of a person's life. This would limit the amount of effect that lifestyle factors could have, and would make it difficult to compare results of studies done on population groups of different ethnic origins.

That's not to say that scientists haven't studied whether lifestyle factors correlate with longevity. Many epidemiologic and animal studies in the exercise and nutrition disciplines have made such attempts, but for one reason or another, they all fall short of absolute proof. Nonetheless, the general trend of results from these studies strongly suggests that lifestyle does affect how long people live.

In the realm of physical activity, various studies comparing the levels of people's long-term occupational and recreational activity, and studies on laboratory animals whose physical activity was regulated, often show longer life for the more physically active individuals. At worst, some studies show no difference; none show shorter lives for the physically active.

A recent study is perhaps the most helpful on the subject (Paffenbarger et al., 1986). Using data collected on approximately 17,000 Harvard alumni, these researchers compared age at death from all causes with the amount of exercise done in the form of walking, stair climbing, and sports play. To quote the findings from the abstract of the study, "Death rates declined steadily as energy expended on such activity increased from less than 500 to 3500 kcal per week, beyond which rates increased slightly. Rates were one-quarter to one-third lower among alumni expending 2000 or more kcal during exercise per week than among less active men."

Comprehensive studies in the realm of nutrition are harder to do, because of the tremendous number of dietary and other variables that would have to be accounted for. In this case, it is more feasible to consider studies that show that particular eating styles can decrease the *incidence* of various diseases; this has been the basis for many of our dietary recommendations in this book. From there, it makes sense to say that if we can reduce the risk of the major causes of death by dietary means, those dietary methods should help extend life.

But what if exercise and good nutriton didn't make much difference in how long we live, after all? Would that sanction the living of a physically lazy and nutritionally careless life?

Not really, unless you're willing to increase your risk of living out your days saddled with chronic disease. Wouldn't it be worth eating healthfully and exercising regularly to have a better chance of feeling good and being unencumbered by disease for more of your life, however long it may be?

We believe it's well worth *living fit*.

Appendix

We have included blank forms of several of the most-used self-checks in this appendix. It may be convenient for you to use them as you continue in your program of living fit.

Self-check 4.2 Estimating activity level and energy expenditure

Activity	Intensity (METS)	Time (hrs/week)	Intensity × time
Eating	1.8		
Sleeping	1.0		
Student, job activities: sitting	1.5		
Active leisure activities:			
Quiet leisure	1.8		
	TOTAL	168	

Your average METS per hour equals the total METS for the week (see the total in column three) divided by 168 (the number of hours per week):

_____ METS/week ÷ 168 hrs/week = _____ METS/hr

Your average energy (kcal) expenditure for a day equals your RMR in kcal/hr (see Self-check 4.1) × 24 hrs per day × your average METS per hour:

_____ kcal/hr × 24 hrs/day × _____ METS/hr = _____ kcal/day

Self-check 7.1   A thoughts diary

An essential part of cognitive restructuring is to discover what you are thinking when you experience stress. You can use this form to determine your stress-producing thoughts.

Time	Situation	Thoughts	Feelings

Self-check 9.1 Documenting your food and nutrient intakes for one day

1. List the foods and amounts you consumed during one day in the first two columns of the form below.
2. Get data for other columns from Table 9.1, adjusting the energy and nutrient values for the size of serving that you actually consumed.
3. If you are using data from food product labels, follow instructions for converting percent of the U.S. RDA into absolute values as described in the text.
4. Determine the total value for each column.

Items consumed	Amount	Energy (kcal)	Protein (grams)	Fat (grams)	Carbohydrate (grams)	Iron (mg)	Calcium (mg)	Sodium (mg)	Vitamin A (IU)	Thiamin (vitamin B-1) (mg)	Riboflavin (vitamin B-2) (mg)	Niacin (mg)	Vitamin C (ascorbic acid) (mg)
Total													

Tr = trace
— = data are unreliable

Self-check 9.2   Calculating what percentages of energy come from protein, fat, and carbohydrate

	Energy (kcal)	Protein (grams)	Fat (gm)	Carbohydrate (grams)	Alcohol (kcal)
1. Transfer values from Self-check 9.1	A[a]				
2. Multiply by kcal/ gram value shown to get energy value		×4	×9	×4	
3. Sum the values in step 2 and record total in space B	B[a] =	+	+		C
4. Divide individual values by total kcalories, which gives decimal fractions					
5. Multiply by 100 to get percentages					

[a]Values in boxes A and B should be within about 25 kcalories of each other. If there is a larger discrepancy, and if there is an alcoholic beverage on the intake record, the extra kcalories are due mainly to the alcohol. To estimate alcohol kcalories, subtract value B from value A and enter the number in box C.

Self-check 9.4   Comparing your actual vitamin and mineral intakes with your recommended dietary allowances or RDAs

	Iron (mg)	Calcium (mg)	Sodium (mg)	Vitamin A (IU)	Thiamin (vitamin B-1) (mg)	Riboflavin (vitamin B-2) (mg)	Niacin (mg)	Vitamin C (ascorbic acid) (mg)
1. Enter totals from Self-check 9.1								
2. Enter RDAs from Table 9.3								
3. Divide totals by RDAs								
4. Multiply by 100 to get percentage								

Self-check 11.1   Recording your eating habits

Time		Place	Food and amount	Alone or with whom	Associated activity	Mood before eating	Hunger 0=none 5=intense	Feeling after eating
Start	End							

Source Notes

Chapter 1: Your health in today's world

Belloc, N.B., and L. Breslow. 1972. Relationship of physical health status and health practices. *Preventive Medicine* 1:409–421.

Belloc, N.B. 1973. Relationship of health practices and mortality. *Preventive Medicine* 2:67–81.

Breslow, L., and J.E. Enstrom. 1980. Persistence of health habits and their relationship to mortality. *Preventive Medicine* 9:469–483.

National Geographic Book Service. 1975. *We Americans*. Washington, D.C.: National Geographic Society.

Chapter 4: How to measure fitness and physical activity

Balke, B. 1963. *A Simple Field Test for the Assessment of Physical Fitness*. CARI report 63-6. Oklahoma City Civil Aeronautical Research Institute, Federal Aviation Agency, April 1963.

Cooper, K.H. 1970. *The New Aerobics*. New York: M. Evans and Co., Inc.

Klissouras, V., F. Pirnay, and J.M. Petit. 1973. Adaptation to maximal effort: Genetics and age. *Journal of Applied Physiology* 35:228–293.

Montoye, H.J., R. Gayle, and M. Higgins. 1980. Smoking habits, alcohol consumption and maximal oxygen uptake. *Medicine and Science in Sports and Exercise* 12:316–321.

Wells, C.L. 1985. *Women, Sport, and Performance: A Physiological Perspective*. Champaign, IL: Human Kinetics Publishers, Inc.

Chapter 5: Exercise programs for fitness

American College of Sports Medicine. 1978. Position Statement on: Recommended Quantity and Quality of Exercise for Developing and Maintaining Fitness in Healthy Adults. *Medicine and Science in Sports and Exercise* 10:vii–x.

Martin, J.E., and P.M. Dubbert. 1985. Adherence to exercise. *Exercise and Sport Sciences Reviews* 13:137–167.

Chapter 7: Dealing with stress

Benson, H. 1975. *The Relaxation Response*. New York: William Morrow. (Also available in paperback.)

Davis, M., E.R. Eshelman, and M. McKay. 1980. *The Relaxation and Stress Reduction Workbook*. Richmond, CA: New Harbinger.

Griest, J.H., M.H. Klein, R.R. Eischens, J. Faris, A.S. Gurman, and W.P. Morgan. 1979. Running as treatment for depression. *Comprehensive Psychiatry* 20:41–53.

McKay, M., M.Davis, and P.Fanning. 1981. *Thoughts and Feelings: The Art of Cognitive Stress Intervention*. Richmond, CA: New Harbinger.

Chapter 10: Food for health, performance, and pleasure

Costill, D.L. 1982. Fats and carbohydrates as determinants of athletic performance. In *Nutrition and Athletic Performance: Proceedings of the Conference on Nutritional Determinants in Athletic Performance*, ed.W. Haskell, J. Scala, and J. Whittam. Palo Alto, CA: Bull Publishing Company.

Chapter 11: Weight control: of lifetime value

Keesey, R.E., and S.W. Corbett. 1984. Metabolic defense of the body weight set-point. In *Eating and Its Disorders*, eds. A.J. Stunkard and E. Stellar. New York: Raven Press.

Lohman, G.T. 1981. Skinfolds and body density and their relation to body fatness: A review. *Human Biology* 53:181–225.

Montoye, H.J., E.L. Smith, D.F. Fardon, and E.T. Howley. 1980. Bone mineral in senior tennis players. *Scandinavian Journal of Sports Sciences* 2:26–32.

Ruderman, A.J. 1986. Dietary restraint: a theoretical and empirical review. *Psychological Bulletin* 99: 247–262.

Williams, M.H. 1985. *Nutritional Aspects of Human Physical and Athletic Performance*. Springfield, IL: Charles C. Thomas.

Chapter 12: Cardiovascular disease: reducing your risk

American Heart Association. 1986. *Dietary Guidelines for Healthy Americans*: A statement for physicians and health professionals by the Nutrition Committee, American Heart Association (AHA). Dallas, TX: AHA.

Committee on Lowering Blood Cholesterol to Prevent Heart Disease. 1985. *Lowering Blood Cholesterol to Prevent Heart Disease*. Bethesda, MD: The National Institutes of Health.

Food and Drug Administration. 1984. *A Word About Low-Sodium Diets*. Rockville, MD: U.S. Department of Health and Human Services.

Friedman, M., and R.H. Rosenman. 1974. *Type A Behavior and Your Heart*. Greenwich, CT: Fawcett Publications, Inc.

Friedman, M., C.E. Thoresen, J.J. Gill, L.H. Powell, D. Ulmer, L. Thompson, V.A. Price, D.D. Rabin, W.S. Breall, R. Dixon, R. Levy, and E. Bourg. 1984. Alteration of Type A behavior and reduction in cardiac recurrences in post-myocardial infarction patients. *American Heart Journal* 108:237–248.

Jenkins, C.D., S.J. Zyzanski, and R.H. Rosenman. 1979. *Jenkins Activity Survey*. New York, N.Y.: Harcourt Brace Jovanovich, Inc.

Kannel, W.B., P. Wilson, and S.N. Blair. 1985. Epidemiological assessment of the role of physical activity and fitness in development of cardiovascular disease. *American Heart Journal* 109:876–885.

Kromhout, D., E.B. Bosschieter, and C. Coulander. 1985. The inverse relation between fish consumption and 20-year mortality from coronary heart disease. *The New England Journal of Medicine* 312:1205–1209.

LaPorte, R.E., L.L. Adams, D.D. Savage, G. Brenes, S. Dearwater, and T. Cook. 1984. The spectrum of physical activity, cardiovascular disease and health: An epidemiologic perspective. *American Journal of Epidemiology* 120:507–517.

Paffenbarger, R.S., R.T. Hyde, A.L. Wing, and C.H. Steinmetz. 1984. A natural history of athleticism and cardiovascular health. *Journal of the American Medical Association* 252:491–495.

Review Panel on Coronary-Prone Behavior and Coronary Heart Disease. 1981. Coronary-prone behavior and coronary heart disease. A critical review. *Circulation* 63:1199.

Rosenman, R.H., M. Friedman, R. Straus, M. Wurm, R. Kositchek, W. Hahn, and N.T. Werthessen. 1964. A predictive study of coronary heart disease: The western collaborative group study. *Journal of the American Medical Association* 189:15–22.

Siscovick, D., N. Weiss, R. Fletcher, and T. Lasky. 1984. The incidence of primary cardiac arrest during vigorous exercise. *New England Journal of Medicine* 311:874–877.

Chapter 13: Aging healthfully

Committee on Diet, Nutrition, and Cancer. 1982. *Diet, Nutrition, and Cancer.* Washington, DC: National Academy Press.

Consensus Development Panel. 1984. *Osteoporosis*: Consensus Development Conference Statement, Vol. 5 (No. 3). Washington, DC: National Institutes of Health.

Heany, R.P., R.R. Recker, and P.D. Saville. 1978. Menopausal changes in calcium balance performance. *Journal Lab. Clin. Med.* 92:953–963.

Jones, H.H., J.D. Priest, W.C. Hayes, C. Tichenor, and D.A. Nagel. 1977. Humeral hypertrophy in response to exercise. *Journal of Bone and Joint Surgery* 59A:204–208.

Krause, M.V., and L.K. Mahan. 1984. *Food, Nutrition, and Diet Therapy.* St. Louis: The C.V. Mosby Company.

Matkovic, V., K. Kostial, I. Simonovic, et al. 1979. Bone status and fracture rates in two regions of Yugoslavia. *American Journal of Clinical Nutrition* 32:540–549.

Montoye, H.J., E.L. Smith, D.F.Fardon, and E.T. Howley. 1980. Bone mineral in senior tennis players. *Scandinavian Journal of Sports Science* 2:26–32.

National Cancer Institute. 1984. *Diet, Nutrition and Cancer Prevention: A Guide to Food Choices.* Washington, DC: U.S. Department of Health and Human Services.

Paffenbarger, R.S., R.T. Hyde, A.L. Wing, and C.C. Hsieh. 1986. Physical activity, all-cause mortality, and longevity of college alumni. *New England Journal of Medicine* 314:605–613.

Recker, R.R. 1983. Osteoporosis. *Contemporary Nutrition.* Minneapolis, MN: General Mills.

Recker, R.R., and R.P. Heany. 1985. The effect of milk supplements on calcium metabolism, bone metabolism and calcium balance. *American Journal of Clinical Nutrition* 41:254–263.

Sowers, M.F., R.B. Wallace, and J.H. Lemke. 1985. Correlates of mid-radius bone density among postmenopausal women: a community study. *American Journal of Clinical Nutrition* 41:1045–1053.

Credits and Acknowledgments

Self-check 1.1   Public Health Service. 1981. *Health Style: a self test*. DHHS Publication No. (PHS) 81-50155. U.S. Department of Health and Human Services.

Figure 1.1   Center for Disease Control. 1980. *Ten Leading Causes of Death in the United States, 1977*. Atlanta: Center for Disease Control.

Figure 1.3   *Statistical Abstract of the United States*. 1980. 101st edition, p. 796. U.S. Department of Commerce, Bureau of the Census. Washington, D.C.: U.S. Govt. Printing Office.

Figure 1.4   U.S. Department of Agriculture. 1981. *Food consumption, prices, and expenditures*. Statistical Bulletin No. 656. Washington, D.C.: USDA Economics and Statistics Service; Marston, R.M., and N.R. Raper. 1981, 1984, 1985, 1986. *National Food Review* 13, 25, 29, 32.

Figures 3.2, 3.3, 3.4, and 3.6   Spence, A.P., and E. Mason. 1982. *Human Anatomy and Physiology*,3rd edition. Menlo Park, CA: The Benjamin/Cummings Publishing Company.

Figure 3.7   Rushmer, R.F. 1955. *Cardiac Diagnosis, a Physiologic Approach*. Philadelphia: Saunders.

Tables 4.1 and 4.2   Montoye, H.J., and D.E. Lamphiear. 1977. Grip and arm strength in males and females, age 10–69. *Research Quarterly* 48:109–120.

Table 4.3   Hunsicker, P.A., and H.J. Montoye. 1953. *Applied tests and measurements in physical education*. New York: Prentice-Hall, Inc.

Table 4.5   Friermood, H.T. 1967. Volleyball skills contest for Olympic development. In *U.S. Volleyball Association, Annual Official Rules and Reference Guide of the U.S. Volleyball Association*. Berne, IN: USVBA Printer.

Tables 4.8 and 4.9   Reiff, G.G., H.J. Montoye, R.D. Remington, J.A. Napier, H.L. Metzner, and F.H. Epstein. 1967. Assessment of physical activity by questionnaire and interview. *Journal of Sports Medicine and Physical Fitness* 7:135–142.

Figure 4.8   Hodgson, J. L. 1971. Age and aerobic capacity of urban Midwestern males. University of Minnesota: Dissertation.

Figure 4.9   Montoye, H. J., R. Gayle, and M. Higgins. 1980. Smoking habits, alcohol consumption, and maximal oxygen uptake. *Medicine and Science in Sports and Exercise* 12:316–321.

Figure 6.1   Nielsen, M. 1938. Die Regulation der Korpentemperatur bei Muskelarbeit. *Skand. Arch. Physiol.* 79:193.

Table 6.2   The National Dairy Council. 1983. *Food Power*. Rosemont, IL: The National Dairy Council.

Figure 6.2   Lamb, D.R. 1978. *Physiology of Exercise: Responses and Adaptations*. New York: Macmillan.

Table 6.3   Adapted from *Runner's World* 8:28 (1973). Reproduced by permission of the publisher, Rodale Press.

Figure 6.3   Adapted from Buskirk, E.R., J. Kollias, E. Picon-Reatigue, R. Akers, E. Prokop, and P. Baker. 1967. Physiology and performance of track athletes at various altitudes in the United States and Peru. In *International Symposium on the Effects of Altitude on Physical Performance*. North Palm Beach, FL: The Athletic Institute.

Figure 6.4.   U.S. Navy. 1963. *U.S. Navy Diving Manual*. Washington, D.C.: U.S. Government Printing Office.

Table 7.1   Adapted from Holmes, T.H., and R.H. Rahe. 1967. The social readjustment rating scale. *Journal of Psychosomatic Research* 11:213–218.

Tables 8.1, 8.2, 8.3, and 8.4   Christian, J.L., and J.L. Greger. 1985. *Nutrition for Living*. Menlo Park, CA: The Benjamin/Cummings Publishing Company.

Figure 8.1   Adapted from Mertz, W. 1983. The significance of trace elements for health. *Nutrition Today* 18:27. Reproduced with permission of *Nutrition Today* Magazine, Annapolis, MD 21404.

Table 9.1   Adapted from *Nutritive Value of American Foods in Common Units*, Agriculture Handbook No. 456, USDA; data for choclate chip cookies, hamburger, lasagna, low-fat milk, and tortilla from Pennington, J.A.T., and H.N. Church. 1985. *Food Values of Portions Commonly Used*, 14th edition. Philadelphia: J.B. Lippincott Co.

Tables 9.4 and 9.5   Adapted from the National Research Council. 1980. *Recommended Dietary Allowances*, ninth edition. Washington, D.C.: National Academy of Sciences.

Figures 10.1–10.6   Adapted from Christian, J.L., and J.L. Greger. 1985. *Nutrition for Living*. Menlo Park, CA: The Benjamin/Cummings Publishing Company.

Table 10.3   Data for athletes from Smith, N. 1976. *Diet for Sport*. Palo Alto, CA: Bull Publishing Company. Data for adult vegetarians from Robertson, L., C. Flanders, and B. Godfrey. 1976. *Laurel's Kitchen* pages 69 and 322. Berkeley: Nilgiri Press. Data for adults with limited budget adapted from Consumer Nutrition Division. 1983. *The Thrifty Food Plan*. Hyattsville, MD: Human Nutrition Information Service, USDA.

Table 10.6   National Association for Sport and Physical Education; the Nutrition Foundation, Inc.; Swanson Center for Nutrition, Inc.; and United States Olympic Committee. 1984. *Nutrition for Sport Success*. Reston, VA: American Alliance for Health, Physical Education, Recreation and Dance.

Table 10.7   Adapted from Clark, Nancy. 1983. *The Athlete's Kitchen*. New York: Bantom Books.

Table 10.8   Christian, J.L., and J.L. Greger. 1985. *Nutrition for Living*. Menlo Park, CA: The Benjamin/Cummings Publishing Company.

Tables 11.1 and 11.2   Adapted from 1983 Metropolitan Height and Weight Tables. Reprinted courtesy of the Metropolitan Life Insurance Company.

Table 12.1   Source: Consensus Development Conference on Lowering Blood Cholesterol to Prevent Heart Disease. 1985. *Lowering blood cholesterol to prevent heart disease*. Bethesda, MD: National Institutes of Health.

Figure 12.1   Adapted from Farrand, M. E., and L. Mojonnier. 1980. Nutrition in the multiple risk factor intervention trial (MRFIT). *Journal of the American Dietetic Association* 76:347–351.

Table 12.2   Adapted from Christian, J.L. and J.L. Greger. 1985. *Nutrition for Living*. Menlo Park, CA: The Benjamin/Cummings Publishing Company.

Table 13.1   Adapted from Christian, J.L., and J.L. Greger. 1985. *Nutrition for Living*. Menlo Park, CA: The Benjamin/Cummings Publishing Company.

Figure 13.1   Garn, S. M., C. G. Rohmann, and B. Wagner. 1967. Bone loss as a general phenomenon in man. *Federation Proceedings* 26:730.

Table 13.2   Adapted from National Cancer Institute. 1984. *Diet, Nutrition, and Cancer Prevention: A guide to food choices*. NIH Publication No. 85-2711. Washington, D.C.: U.S. Dept. of Health and Human Services.

Figure 13.2   Garn, S. M. 1970. *The Earlier Gain and the Later Loss of Cortical Bone*. Springfield, IL: Charles C. Thomas.